Rhythms

of

Faith, Hope & Grace

52 Devotional Poems

Sulekha Esther Rathnam

INDIA · SINGAPORE · MALAYSIA

Credit:-

All the Biblical texts are taken from the English Standard Version Bible - https://www.biblegateway.com/versions/English-Standard-Version-ESV-Bible/

Rhythms of Faith, Hope & Grace

is a collection of poetry based on Scripture.

In Loving Memory

Of

My Father - C.S. Rathnam – who challenged me to memorise scripture and to pursue writing (May 2020)

My Best Friend - Raynold Manuel – who was my one man cheerleading squad, and believed I could do anything. He wanted me to publish a book! (Aug 2021)

My Darling Niece - Ava Rathnam – who had me dream, love, ache, and write again (Feb 2024)

My Godmother - Ranjini Cabral – who inspired me, loved me, and spurred me on (July 2017)

My Uncle – Romesh Ignatius – who was a talented writer himself and encouraged me to keep writing (Dec 2017).

All of these people meant the world to me, and their loss made me exercise my faith!

THANK YOU

to

Rhoda Rathnam, my mother, who has wanted this to happen for years and has never stopped encouraging me and who made me treasure scripture,

To my brother, **Vishal**, the critic who always provided brutally honest feedback,

and sister-in-law **Amruta** who was kind and patient,

All three of them had to put up with reading all my poems.

To my **Sunday school teachers** in **Madras** and **Pune** for the **Bible lessons**,

To my **Youth Leaders** & **Mentors** who invested in me,

To my **Pastors** in **Madras**, **Pune** & **Hungary**,

To my **church** who reminded me that my writing can be encouragement and

To my **friends** and **extended family** who have stood by me and supported me.

To my school in **Madras - Spartan Matriculation**, for making me memorise scripture and enjoy it and to my **English subject teachers** in **St. Anne's High School - Pune,** for encouraging me to write.

I am blessed, and I can only hope that it reflects through my writing.

Contents

1. What is Man? 11

2. Who Am I? 13

3. Ambition 15

4. The Other Night 17

5. Obey 19

6. I Hear 21

7. Grace 22

8. Grace, My Debtor 24

9. Stillness 26

10. Be Still 28

11. What's in a Name? 30

12. His Name 32

13. Power in Unity 33

14. Prayer 35

15. O God 36

16. New Beginning 37

17. Dawn 39

18. Dichotomy 41

19. Narrow Road 43

20. Cursed of Twelve 44

21. Judas 46

22. Follow 48

23. I Choose Him 50

24. Our God 53

25. There's a God 55
26. Learning All is His 56
27. Ava 58
28. Tranquillity 60
29. Be Still My Soul! 62
30. Sinner to Saint 64
31. Paul 66
32. Faith-Full? 68
33. Faith 70
34. Appearance 73
35. Reflection 75
36. Wretched Sinner 77
37. The Dying Thief 79
38. Wholehearted Follower 81
39. My Heart's Cry 83
40. Our God, the Greatest Artist 85
41. The Painter 87
42. All Things for Our Good 88
43. Good 90
44. Carved 92
45. 'Tis But Mighty Hands 94
46. I Surrender 95
47. Take it All Away 97
48. Heavenly Abode 99
49. I Wonder 101
50. Pistis 102
51. Faith and Hope 104
52. Golgotha 105
53. Calvary 107

54. Loss 109

55. Goodbye Ava 111

56. Making it Count! 113

57. Marred Image 115

58. Perfect Home 117

59. The Garden of Eden 119

60. Living for Jesus 120

61. On Fire for Jesus 122

62. Safe in the Arms of God 123

63. A Tribute to Ruth 125

64. A Woman's Place 127

65. Esther 129

66. Friend for Sinners 131

67. Have You Met Jesus? 133

68. Paraklesis 135

69. Comfort 137

70. Emunah 138

71. Steadfast Faith 140

72. A Requisition 141

73. Adjuration 143

74. Come Undone 144

75. My Cry 146

76. In His Image 148

77. Cut by the Knife 150

78. Home Away from Home 151

79. Joy in A Foreign Land 153

80. Answered Prayer 155

81. For this Child I Prayed 157

82. Cobbled Streets 159

83. Joyous Heaven 161

84. Go Tell 167

85. Evangelism 169

86. A Pandemic 171

87. Covid19 173

88. Purposeful Life 174

89. Purpose 176

90. Suffering Saint 178

91. Job 180

92. Show Me Your Glory! 182

93. In the Cleft of the Rock 184

94. In His Strength 185

95. Trial 188

96. Power of the Cross 190

97. Cross Hymn 192

98. Refined 193

99. The Promise of Trial 195

100. Seek Ye First 197

101. Treasures in Heaven 199

102. Living Through Loss 200

103. Confessions 202

104. Colours to Cheer 204

105. Rainbow 206

What is Man?

A decade and a half ago, when I was in the youth group, many of us were madly in love with the song "Who Am I" by Casting Crowns. While some of us loved that song, others didn't think the song had too much meaning to it. But to me, the song was always a reminder of Psalm 8, and I decided I needed to write something that reflected what the psalm meant to me. When I was travelling through Manali and admiring the Himalayas, the poem took birth. Have you ever visited the Himalayas? It's vast, beautiful, and simply magnificent. The mountains and the skies seem to almost meet, no matter which window you look out of. One fine evening, while I was sipping on my coffee, I saw the sun set, and I was fascinated by how the snow-clad mountains reflected the colours of the setting sun. Neither picture nor words, can ever do that sunset justice. It was simply magnificent. I marvelled at God's creation, so perfect. I was drawn to worship. It was hard to be in the presence of such beauty and not wonder how Awesome God is. And while I spared all thought to how Awesome God must be, I also realised how insignificant I was. The Himalayas have a great way of making us feel small, literally. Psalm 8 rang loudly in my head and heart, "What is man that you are mindful of him?" Nature has a fine way of making us forget our circumstances and instead worship the creator God, who orchestrated so much beauty into being. If we ever find ourselves in a situation where we feel like we really have nothing to praise God about, all we have to do is look around us, at nature, and a million reasons to praise God will be found.

Psalm 8: - 3-4
When I look at your heavens, the work of your fingers,
The moon and the stars, which you have set in place,
What is man that you are mindful of him?
and the son of man that you care for him?

Genesis 1:27
So God created man in his own image,
in the image of God he created him;
male and female he created them.

2 Corinthians 5:17
Therefore, if anyone is in Christ, he is a new creation. The old has passed away; behold, the new has come.

2 Corinthians 5:21
For our sake, he made him to be sin who knew no sin, so that in him we might become the righteousness of God.

Galatians 3:13
Christ redeemed us from the curse of the law by becoming a curse for us—for it is written, "Cursed is everyone who is hanged on a tree."

Who Am I?

When I look at the heavens above,
It does reflect thy glorious love.
It tells of a marvellous story,
Of a God who reigns in glory.
And then consumed in thought, I ask,
Who am I?

When I look at the stars infinite,
My mortal descriptive words, Ah! so finite!
In the twinkling of the starry host,
I only find thy awesomeness to boast.
Filled with awe and wonder, I ponder,
Who am I?

When I look at all thy bountiful creatures,
Each one unique, in its striking features.
Man, made in your own glorious likeness,
I am gripped by your all-encompassing greatness.
And every heartbeat within me cries,
Who am I?

When I look into thy word, in absolute silence,
Mine eyes behold the Holy Lamb, victim of Calvary's violence.

Holiness clothed with, my dreadful, impending sin,
The Lamb's resurrection, my perfect, righteous, eternal win.
Clothed in holiness, justified through Christ, I stand humbled,
Who am I?

Ambition

When I visited friends in America, I accompanied them to their kids' class for mathematics and science, and as we waited, I noticed that every kid that came out from that class was either Indian or from an Asian country. It really is so ingrained in our Indian culture to pursue education. Every conversation with an adult, when we were kids, was about our future education. In fact, it is the only small talk, most adults indulge in with kids. It is common for mere acquaintances to inquire about our grades. Education is of utmost importance; it is drilled into us since we were kids. Every parent dreams of a Master's, PhD, medical degree, engineering degree, or more, for their child. It isn't okay to be mediocre; one ought to be ambitious. Every parent wants their kid to become someone relevant, and every child grows up believing education is the only thing that defines them. Even Christian parents make the same mistake and mimic the world. The Bible teaches us, we are nothing; our identity ought to be found in nothing else, but Christ. Our goal, our aim, our focus, ought to be, to be Christlike! Education and ambition are good, but not when they take precedence over God in our lives. Every Christian is called to but one goal: Christlikeness and to bring him glory! Paul is a fantastic example of treasuring what's really important! Despite his prestigious academic accomplishments, he tells us he counts all of it as loss, in comparison to the surpassing greatness, of knowing Christ. Paul tells us nothing comes close to Christ!

Philippians 3:8-14

Indeed, I count everything as loss because of the surpassing worth of knowing Christ Jesus my Lord. For his sake, I have suffered the loss of all things and count them as rubbish, in order that I may gain Christ and be found in him, not having a righteousness of my own that comes from the law, but that which comes through faith in Christ, the righteousness from God that depends on faith— that I may know him and the power of his resurrection, and may share his sufferings, becoming like him in his death, that by any means possible I may attain the resurrection from the dead. Not that I have already obtained this or am already perfect, but I press on to make it my own, because Christ Jesus has made me his own. Brothers, I do not consider that I have made it my own. But one thing I do: forgetting what lies behind and straining forward to what lies ahead, I press on toward the goal for the prize of the upward call of God in Christ Jesus.

2 Corinthians 10:17

"Let the one who boasts, boast in the Lord."

The Westminster Shorter Catechism says that *"Man's chief end is to glorify God, and to enjoy him forever."*

The Other Night

The Other night, as I lay on my bed,
A crazy thought, ran through my head.

What if I never wake tomorrow?
Would I be the cause of pain and sorrow?

I continued to lie, in pensive thought,
While I made a list of things in life, I sought.

I sought family, friends, money, and fame,
My only goal, to build me a name.

I even sought the thrills of love,
But failed miserably, to seek my Father above.

Suddenly my funeral flashed before my eyes,
I heard people share kind words, but alas all lies!

My twenty-two years seemed futile on earth,
For Christlikeness within me, was still taking birth.

These people thought, that they did know me,
I was more sinful, than they ever could see.

The thought of my life wasted and spent,
Shook me up and made me repent.

No longer was I in pensive thought,
Gripped by reality, righteousness I sought.

It took one night on my rickety old bed,
To make me realise, what lies for me ahead.

Today I live, not anymore, my name to lift,
But to a world of lost sinners, Christ to gift.

I strive to let, my actions do the talking,
Hoping one day my funeral, won't be a mocking.

I wish not in death, to leave a name,
Just Christ and his eternal riches, for others to claim.

Obey

I love being Indian; there's some fascinating things about our culture that you don't find elsewhere. We live out hospitality, we teach kids to respect elders, books, and even strangers and honour them with "Uncle" and "Aunty" too. Growing up in Madras, we were a tight community of a few families. We were a set of folks who went to the same church; everyone's kids went to the same school, and everyone's kids were best friends with each other. In this community, often enough, someone would run into another's house, to borrow sugar or salt or send their kids over to ask for it, because it was easier to get it from someone's home instantly than run over to a store. Of course, today we have Swiggy, Zepto, and the likes, but we didn't have that back in the 90s when I was growing up. No matter who borrowed what, they'd never return your bowl, empty. Treats would always accompany the bowl, because in Indian culture, you never return a bowl or dish, empty; it must be filled. Some of us come to God thinking the same! We can't go empty-handed! We meet him at the cross and think, I'll return the favour by going to church every Sunday; I need to give something back to him. Funny that we should even dare to think that, don't you think? What could we possibly give to the one who owns all things, including us? The cross actually teaches us just that; we have nothing worthy to give him. Every good deed we can think of doing is but a filthy rag in his sight. We can bring no good to God unless he has already ordained it for us! There is no good deed we do that isn't already orchestrated by him. The only right response to Calvary is, Lord here, have my life, unworthy, empty as it is, fill it with what's pleasing to you! Submission through obedience, is all we have, to give God! Our obedience, God counts as love, and that pleases him above all else!

Isaiah 64:6
We have all become like one who is unclean,
And all our righteous deeds are like a polluted garment.
We all fade like a leaf,
And our iniquities, like the wind, take us away.

1 John 3: 23-24
And this is his commandment, that we believe in the name of his Son Jesus Christ and love one another, just as he has commanded us. Whoever keeps his commandments abides in God, and God in him. And by this we know that he abides in us, by the Spirit whom he has given us.

Ephesians 2:10
For we are his workmanship, created in Christ Jesus for good works, which God prepared beforehand, that we should walk in them.

I Hear

I hear my precious Saviour say,
No more, for sin, do you need to pay.
He cleared my very sinful debt, O Lord, how could I ever you repay?
He whispered to me, soft and clear, "My child, just my word obey."

I hear my Saviour talk to me,
When the storms are near, and I feel at sea.
He tells me not to ever fret, for he, my guide, to the end will be.
I know it's true, I find him near, each time I come on bended knee.

I hear my risen Saviour call me "Dear".
It fills my heart with joy, yet grips me with fear.
This almighty, holy, righteous God, who my every sin did clear,
Will one day sit at judgement seat and hear my account for every year.

Grace

Our Christian definition of "grace" is a beautiful one! We say grace is the unmerited gift of God's favour, and indeed it is. Undeserving sinners like us, receive grace and become children of God, children who have a share in his inheritance and heavenly home. While grace is beautiful, many of us misuse it, take it for granted, abuse it, and spend it. But what a great Father we have, who is able to give us, more than we need! So when we recognise our misuse of his grace and come back, asking for more, He still blesses us with grace.

If you're reading this and thinking, I've done this so many times before, you're not alone. Recognising we've misused "grace" is only part of making it right! The other involves never repeating it again. All we need to do is, approach his throne of grace, in repentance and truth. He will honour a heartfelt request and bless us, with forgiveness and more grace, than we deserve. Our God is a gracious God, and every story recorded in the Bible, is an example of it; from Abraham to Jesus' disciples, we see the abundance of grace poured out, on each of them. Such, is the grace we have access to, that is, everyone who believes in Christ Jesus.

Ephesians 2:8
For by grace you have been saved through faith. And this is not your own doing; it is the gift of God.

Romans 7:18

For I know that nothing good dwells in me, that is, in my flesh. For I have the desire to do what is right, but not the ability to carry it out.

Romans 6:1-2

What shall we say then? Are we to continue in sin that grace may abound? By no means! How can we who died to sin still live in it?

1 John 1:9

If we confess our sins, he is faithful and just to forgive us our sins and to cleanse us from all unrighteousness.

Hebrews 10:19-22

Therefore, brothers, since we have confidence to enter the holy places by the blood of Jesus, by the new and living way that he opened for us through the curtain, that is, through his flesh,[21] and since we have a great priest over the house of God, let us draw near with a true heart in full assurance of faith, with our hearts sprinkled clean from an evil conscience and our bodies washed with pure water.

Grace, My Debtor

Oh! So far away from him, did I stray!
Sin, glittering on my path and way.
Filled with choices of blatant unrighteousness,
I took every step, in full consciousness.
But even in the depths of my newfound darkness,
A soft voice spoke of his forgiveness and gifted righteousness.
But I continued with ugly sin and self,
Shutting down the voice that spoke of Christ himself.
I filled life with self and want,
Did wicked things without daunt.
And even in fulfilling all my want,
I stood there discontent, for something did haunt.
It was the cross, that blood-stained cross,
that often seized my thoughts while I did lie.
It spoke of him, the one whom for sinners did die!
He didn't live for self or want,
He died, so sin could no longer me, haunt.
I did my best to shake that thought out of my head,
For I knew sin, let me stray way ahead.
But that cross, it never did leave me,
Brought me back to him, on bended knee.
For all my fulfilment, of want and sin,
Never did peace, joy, or calm, ever win.
Sin led to momentary joy, yet deep unrest,
It never gave peace or joy, a home or nest.

I dreaded that cross, that flashed upon my eye,
For it reminded me that eternally damned was I!
Until one day, that which haunted me, became my hope,
I remembered how that thief upon the cross, with his sin did
cope.
I had taken a million steps away, from my God.
But not a step too far, for my sovereign Lord.
Righteousness was never something, I could earn,
This now, something, I did truly learn.
For nothing in me, was ever worthy, to make me his,
T'was only grace that saved me and ever made me his.
For I can never choose to be, all righteousness,
For I live in a body, that's cursed with sinfulness.
But in Christ, I can choose to live, righteously!
For covered in his blood, my sin has been dealt with, justly.
So, though stray I did, far, far away,
By grace, I am forgiven, his forever and today!

Stillness

"Be still," if you've grown up in a Christian home, you've probably heard that many times and also might I add, completely out of context. Parents freely say "Be still" and Christianise it by saying the Bible says so also. What is being still? It is almost literally what it says, staying still. But this "stillness" is rooted in our faith. It is the stillness that can only come from a heart that knows "God is in control," and it's not as easy as it sounds. It is easy to trust God when everything is swell. It is extremely hard to believe God is in control, when terrible things happen. It is easier to think God wasn't watching because otherwise, we have to come to terms with understanding that this Sovereign God ordains both, good and the not-so-good in our lives. How can this be? is usually the question that haunts us.

The next poem was born from grief, while I mourned my niece. Those who know me know, there's nothing on earth I love more than children. I have babysat more kids than I can ever count. Even in foreign lands, I have befriended strangers' kids and played with them. Some people say I have magic, some call me the child whisperer, others the Pied Piper of children. Being single, above the so-called marriageable age, and a terrible diabetic, almost guarantees that I will never personally know that joy. So the joy of having a niece or nephew was beyond what my pen can ever tell you. I was ecstatic. Also, a bitter lesson I recently learnt was, you can love someone else's kids like they are your own, but they will always remain someone else' kids. I am very grateful to the friends that have let me love their kids and continue to let me do so; it fills my heart with more joy than they will ever know, and this being my brother's kid, I was sure it would be different, I was sure I'd have lifetime access to this kid! I remember often saying "Finally", one that's "Mine". But joy soon turned to great, deep, heart- wrenching sorrow, when my niece was born sleeping (stillborn). It's been a few months now and the memory of that day is still vivid in my mind. "Be still" was born from that grief.

Psalm 46 and Lamentations 3 helped me.

Psalm 46:10-11
"Be still, and know that I am God.
I will be exalted among the nations,
I will be exalted in the earth!"
The Lord of hosts is with us;
the God of Jacob is our fortress.

Lamentations 3:21-23
But this I call to mind,
and therefore I have hope:
The steadfast love of the Lord never ceases;
his mercies never come to an end;
they are new every morning;
great is your faithfulness.

Be Still

Be still, you said, know I am God,
But how do I do that, dear Lord?
The winds are raging and roaring around.
I know not how, to stand my ground!

Be still, you said, know I am God,
And how am I supposed to do that, Lord?
When the waters I am in are rough and wild,
How am I to remember, I am your child?

Be still, you said, know I am God,
And when do I do that, Lord?
When the hours keep rolling with burdens and cares,
And my heart's tired, with all its aches and wears!

Be still, you said, know I am God,
I am trying, but terribly failing, Lord.
Even in the silence, it's not your voice I hear,
It's the echo of regret, doubt, fears, and tears!

Be still, you said, know I am God,
So I'll go to where you said that, Lord,
In your word, I finally find a comfort, I can't explain,
Despite the chaos that surrounds, peace remains.

Be still, you said, know I am God,
For that directive, I thank you, Lord.
No matter what shall come my way,
Stayed upon Jehovah, my heart shall be blessed, every day!

What's in a Name?

We live in crazy times where names are increasingly daft. Creativity, or the lack of creativity, has given birth to some absurd names. While I don't look forward to hearing new names these days, I have always been fascinated by the names in the Bible. The names meant something; in fact, most often, they indicated the character or characteristics of a person. Adam – son of earth, Eve – life, Abraham – Father of many, Isaac – one who laughs, Jacob – Jehovah shall add, Israel – God preserves, YHWH (Yahweh) – I am what I am, is the biblical meaning and other scholars over the years have tried coming up with a definition and most agree on "He brings into existence whatever exists (Yahweh-Asher-Yahweh).

Jesus, the name we Christians live by, the meaning of it is "The Lord is salvation," and how true indeed it is! It is through Jesus that we have salvation. The Bible teaches us that this name is to be revered; it belongs to one who is holy, loved by God the Father, and who brings salvation to man.

Exodus 20:7
"You shall not take the name of the Lord your God in vain, for the Lord will not hold him guiltless who takes his name in vain."

Matthew 1:21
She will bear a son, and you shall call his name Jesus, for he will save his people from their sins.

John 14:6

Jesus said to him, "I am the way, and the truth, and the life. No one comes to the Father except through me."

Philippians 2: 9-11

Therefore, God has highly exalted him and bestowed on him the name that is above every name, so that at the name of Jesus every knee should bow, in heaven and on earth and under the earth, and every tongue confess that Jesus Christ is Lord, to the glory of God the Father.

His Name

Oh, the name of Jesus, how blessed it is,
In thy sorrow, great joy it gives.

That name so powerful, all sin forgives,
And to lost sinners, new life it gives.

His name though old, no power shall lose,
For by it, people, still life will choose.

So sing that name, forever more,
Until you reach, his heavenly shore.

And even in heaven above,
His name will always, ring of love.

As sweet as heaven, will prove to be,
His name will still, far sweeter be.

Power in Unity

We all understand power in unity, strength in numbers and yet somehow, we forget that in our Christian walk. We are always trying to do it on our own; what's worse, we try to do it without God himself. For some reason, we want to fit ourselves for heaven, the same heaven we already know, we can never reach without Christ. Quite silly our actions, isn't it? Also, we must recognise, salvation on this side of heaven still has us, in sinful bodies, which, like Paul says, continues to make us do things against God, that we don't want to do. It would be foolish of us to think, of resisting evil on our own. We need Jesus! We need God's word. We need to spend time at his throne of grace, in prayer. "Near to the heart of God" is one of my favourite hymns by McAfee and what richness he provides in his lyrics. *"There is a place of quiet rest, near to the heart of God, a place where sin cannot molest, Near to the heart of God"*. Our best shot at fighting sin, is staying near God. Sin loses its power when Jesus is near. To live our Christian life and to live it to its fullest, we need Christ! Without Christ, there is no Christian life that can be lived.

James 4:7-8
Submit yourselves therefore to God. Resist the devil, and he will flee from you. Draw near to God, and he will draw near to you. Cleanse your hands, you sinners, and purify your hearts, you double-minded.

John 16:24

Until now, you have asked nothing in my name. Ask, and you will receive, that your joy may be full.

2 Corinthians 12:9-10

But he said to me, "My grace is sufficient for you, for my power is made perfect in weakness." Therefore, I will boast all the more gladly of my weaknesses, so that the power of Christ may rest upon me. For the sake of Christ, then, I am content with weaknesses, insults, hardships, persecutions, and calamities. For when I am weak, then I am strong.

Prayer

Be thou, O Lord, my every thought,
In waking or in sleep.

Be thou, O Lord, my only song,
Through both, joy and grief.

Naught be thou, far from me Lord,
Or life, will sinful be.

But be thou, O Lord, by my side,
Till one day heaven I reach.

O God

In my sorrow, many tears they fall,
Drenched and weary, on you I call.
Not seeking faces, just your grace,
I need your love, your Fatherly embrace.

In my loneliness, no one I want,
Away from people and all their chant,
Just peace and quiet, is all I claim,
Grant it O Lord, in thy blessed name.

In my weakness, no strength I find,
Completely hopeless, my state of mind.
But in thy strength, renewed I rise,
Fit to fight and win that prize.

In my life, nothing more I'll ask,
Be thou my guide, in every task.
N'er leave me, or like sheep I'll stray,
My life will be in vain, your calling, I'll betray

New Beginning

Everyone either directly had something terrible happen to them, their friends or family, during Covid. I lost my Dad in the heart of Covid. To most children, this loss is devastating, but my Dad and I, we didn't share the common parent-child relationship. My parents split when I was 9, and since then I never lived with my Dad. Our relationship was more complicated than I care to share. But death, that's final, no wonder they say, "the last nail in the coffin." So hearing my Dad died and not having the opportunity to attend his funeral or lay him in the grave, was a pain I can't quite tell you about. For all the fights we had, for all the silence we chose to live in, I thought saying "goodbye" would be easier, but it wasn't. Death has this unique way of making everything else seem terribly trivial. The birthdays he missed, the rude calls, the difficult letters, the tough holidays, they seemed so easy to forget. The laughs, the silly voices he made, the hugs he gave, the compliments he paid, the bedtime stories he shared, all of them suddenly loud in my head and memories. I missed my Dad with an aching heart. It was in the midst of all this ache and pain that the words from yet another favourite hymn by Frances Ridley Havergal came to mind: *Stayed upon Jehovah hearts are fully blest, finding as he promised perfect peace and rest,*" and I knew this came from Isaiah 26. As I was meditating on this, I was led to Lamentations 3. I was listening to a sermon by Alistair Begg, and I loved what he pointed out; he said the author of Lamentations was saying, "this I recall, I call to mind," meaning it wasn't something that came naturally; he exercised a memory. In the midst of my sorrow, I was reminded that while I had nothing to "joy" in right now, it would do me good to "recall" the days I had things to "joy" in because of the loving kindness of my God. Strangely, the last song my Dad sent me to listen to was "My life is in your hands" (by Maverick City Music, Chandler Moore, and Kirk Franklin), another reminder of who I should be finding comfort in.

Isaiah 26:3-4
You keep him in perfect peace
whose mind is stayed on you,
because he trusts in you.
Trust in the Lord forever,
for the Lord God is an everlasting rock.

Lamentations 3:21-25
But this I call to mind,
and therefore I have hope:
The steadfast love of the Lord never ceases;
His mercies never come to an end;
They are new every morning;
Great is your faithfulness.
"The Lord is my portion," says my soul,
"Therefore, I will hope in him."
The Lord is good to those who wait for him,
to the soul who seeks Him.

Dawn

A new dawn has come to Earth,
Another year is taking birth.
And Lord, here I am grieving.
Over all that was and what could have been!
But days you've numbered.
Ought to be more than these, Lord,
Days you've numbered.
Ought to be more of you, and less of me.
Days you've numbered.
Ought to be shaping me, into you.

So teach me, Lord, when dawn arises,
To look not at marred image or
My ugly reflection,
But to trace your compassion,
In the promise of new day,
For your compassions, they never fail,
They are new every morning.
And should I be led to lament, Lord,
Help me recall, bring back to mind.
Great is your faithfulness, O Lord,
It's sweeter than my deepest pain,
It's brighter than the rising sun!
It's my hope for every morrow.

Let me never forget, O Lord,
Your loving kindness can never cease.
The Lord does not reject forever,
For He who allows grief,
Does give compassion,
In accordance with his rich kindness.
So in this hope, Lord, let me embrace new day,
Knowing, that my numbered days, shall only have your way!

Dichotomy

Life is full of choices; the only time we are spared of them, is when we are kids. But once adolescence kicks in, we are plagued with having to make decisions. The older we grow, the more decisions we need to make and often enough, we are given the dangerous authority of having to make decisions for others. One of the biggest decisions any of us will ever have to make is, the dichotomy of whether to follow Christ or not. Every single individual who walks this planet is given this choice. We must either choose to follow Christ or reject him. The Bible tells us in Matthew 7, there are two gates, one leading up a narrow road and the other, a wide one. The narrow road is less travelled on, the wide one, sees many but what awaits them is destruction. If you are wise, you will choose the narrow road; it leads to Christ. There's a reason why the narrow gate isn't attractive; it is paved with difficulty. When we embrace Christ, we embrace all that he was and is, meaning we embrace suffering, just like he did.

Matthew 7:13-14
"Enter by the narrow gate. For the gate is wide and the way is easy that leads to destruction, and those who enter by it are many. For the gate is narrow and the way is hard that leads to life, and those who find it are few."

Romans 5:1-5

Therefore, since we have been justified by faith, we have peace with God through our Lord Jesus Christ. Through him, we have also obtained access by faith into this grace in which we stand, and we rejoice in hope of the glory of God. Not only that, but we rejoice in our sufferings, knowing that suffering produces endurance, and endurance produces character, and character produces hope, and hope does not put us to shame because God's love has been poured into our hearts through the Holy Spirit who has been given to us.

1 Peter 2:21

For to this you have been called, because Christ also suffered for you, leaving you an example, so that you might follow in his steps.

Romans 8:16-17

The Spirit himself bears witness with our spirit that we are children of God, and if children, then heirs—heirs of God and fellow heirs with Christ, provided we suffer with him in order that we may also be glorified with him.

Narrow Road

Teach me, Lord, this day, I pray,
Ne'er to want or walk that broad way.
For worldly pleasures, I shall surely find,
But shall ne'er own, thy heart or mind.
But that narrow road, to thy home doth lead,
This I know, thy word does teach.
So keep thou me, on that path, I plead!
Until thy heavenly home, I one day reach.
And though that path be, narrow and steep,
Help me, each step, thy faith, to keep.
Let me ne'er fail, test or trial,
Teach me, all things cometh, from thy dial.
For trials, Lord, may I ever long,
Then to me, perseverance shall belong.
Character, I shall then find, by grace,
And hope shall fill me with thy face.
So give me, Lord, what thou must give,
To let me, like Christ, here live.
May the world, in me, see thy light,
As I walk humbly, in faith, and not by sight.
And when at last, I'm put to dust,
May my testimony be,
I lived as every Christian must!

Cursed of Twelve

Judas Iscariot is a name that won't ever be forgotten in history. His name will always ring of betrayal. To be chosen by Jesus, live with Jesus, be loved by Jesus and then betray him would take a certain kind of strength and lack of character in a man. Let's not forget, Jesus wasn't just a man; Jesus was the long-awaited messiah of the Jews. He was the Son of God, and his disciples accepted him as that, yet Judas betrayed him. Is there anything to be learnt from Judas' life? So much, so very much! Consider this: for the 3 years of his ministry on earth, Jesus spent the maximum time with his disciples. Judas was one of these twelve, a chosen disciple. Jesus handpicked these twelve disciples; He gave them the power to perform miracles. Judas enjoyed this privilege like every other disciple. Also, a few places in the Bible have it recorded for us that Jesus says, "one of you will betray me," and it's not like anyone could guess it would be Judas, which meant he probably blended in well with the disciples. Judas seemed like one of the 12; he did what the others did, he went where the others went, he served like the others served, but he betrayed Jesus. What can we learn from Judas? We can pretend to be a follower of Jesus but actually betray him. We can all become like Judas if we let other interests take over our heart rather than Jesus. We may go to church, serve at ministries, and be part of mission trips, but we could still find ourselves not in his flock, if our heart isn't given fully to Jesus. Judas betrayed Jesus for money. In essence, he considered money, better than Jesus. We need to examine our hearts and see: does

Jesus occupy our heart or do worldly things occupy it? Judas betrayed Jesus but couldn't live with what he had done; the money brought no fulfilment, and he gave it back, but he could not undo betraying Jesus. We need to be careful; if we let sin dwell in our hearts, it could consume us, overtake us, and cause us to betray the one who gave us life anew - Jesus.

Matthew 10:1
And he called to him his twelve disciples and gave them authority over unclean spirits to cast them out and to heal every disease and every affliction.

John 13:-21-22
After saying these things, Jesus was troubled in his spirit and testified, "Truly, truly, I say to you, one of you will betray me." The disciples looked at one another, uncertain of whom he spoke.

Matthew 7:21
"Not everyone who says to me, 'Lord, Lord,' will enter the kingdom of heaven, but the one who does the will of my Father who is in heaven."

Matthew 27:3-5
Then when Judas, his betrayer, saw that Jesus was condemned, he changed his mind and brought back the thirty pieces of silver to the chief priests and the elders, saying, "I have sinned by betraying innocent blood." They said, "What is that to us? See to it yourself." And throwing down the pieces of silver into the temple, he departed, and he went and hanged himself.

Judas

Jesus chose a special twelve,
With him, to follow and dwell.
He loved them oh! So truly,
Even though he knew one would betray him severely.
With the seal of a kiss,
One would end this earthly bliss.
This Oh! so cursed one,
Would betray the Father's beloved Son.
Thirty silver coins he claimed,
For the Son of Man, whom our sins would reclaim.
But guilt would flood his heart and soul,
His blood would spill, his betrayal forever told.
Judas, the name of that wretched soul,
Betrayal, his cursed, sinful role.
One, among the precious twelve,
Yet eternally with Christ, he shall never dwell.
After committing that dreadful crime,
His conscience with guilt did chime.
Unable to bear the cost of his sin,
To death he hung, he had nothing to lose, nothing to win.
Sin my friend, shall always bear its weight,
But in Christ, there's relief; it's never too late.
Judas died in guilt and sin,
You, in Jesus, life and righteousness can win.

So deny yourself today, your old self and sin,
At Calvary, find blood that was shed, your pardon to win.
Choose this day, with Christ to dwell,
Be not like Judas, the cursed of twelve.

Follow

We are all given the command to follow, all of us who believe in Jesus Christ. The command to follow that is given, to us Christians, is not circumstantial; we are called to follow when it's easy, when it's hard, when it's difficult, and even when, the cross seems impossible to bear. We are called to follow at all times. The Christian walk demands a commitment to Christ; this commitment is to walk with Christ, regardless of what is happening around. Now, while that might seem like too tall an order to abide by, Christ gives us what we need, to follow through. The Bible tells us that while we attempt what seems like an impossible task, God will give us the strength to do it. He also promises never to give us more than we can bear. Furthermore, God promises in his word that he will never leave us nor forsake us. So then, is this walk really hard? Yes, it is! It is a hard walk; temptation will surround us, loss will weaken our stride, sin will make heavy, our every step, but with Christ with us, we will be able to walk in his step. The decision to follow Christ is not a one-time choice alone; it is an everyday choice we keep making, till the day we die. Every day, in our "following" we will need to make that choice of "Christ" over "everything else," and as we do that, we will find his promises ever near and dear. Soon, not only will we be following but making followers too.

Deuteronomy 31:8
It is the Lord who goes before you. He will be with you; he will not leave you or forsake you. Do not fear or be dismayed.

Mark 8:34
And calling the crowd to him with his disciples, he said to them, "If anyone would come after me, let him deny himself and take up his cross and follow me."

Luke 9:23-24
And he said to all, "If anyone would come after me, let him deny himself and take up his cross daily and follow me." "For whoever would save his life will lose it, but whoever loses his life for my sake will save it."

1 John 2 :3-6
And by this, we know that we have come to know him if we keep his commandments. Whoever says "I know him" but does not keep his commandments is a liar, and the truth is not in him, but whoever keeps his word, in him truly the love of God is perfected. By this, we may know that we are in him: whoever says he abides in him ought to walk in the same way in which he walked.

Hebrews 3:12-14
Take care, brothers, lest there be in any of you an evil, unbelieving heart, leading you to fall away from the living God. But exhort one another every day, as long as it is called "today," that none of you may be hardened by the deceitfulness of sin. For we have come to share in Christ, if indeed we hold our original confidence firm to the end.

I Choose Him

You know not of the cross I bear,
You only know of what, I wish to share.
But, there within me, lies a measureless void,
What no one can quench, something I cannot avoid.
Hollow, though my heart has been,
He has, my every deed seen.
And now, he holds my trembling hand,
Leads me to his promise land.

O Brother, I cannot leave his hand,
He who, from the miry clay,
On a rock, made me stand.
When my steps were aweary,
And the world, from me did stray,
O Brother! He, my Saviour, carried me all the way.

We only know, what life can give,
We know not what, death can bring.
And the unknown shall always, be our fear,
For we know not how, for it to gear.
Would it be a surprise or would it be a shock,
The answers, who shall ever unlock?
And through the doubt, I feel a steady hand,
Comforting me onward, to that Promised Land.

O Sister, I cannot leave his hand,
He who, from the miry clay,
On a rock, made me stand.
When my steps were aweary,
And the world, from me did stray,
O Sister! He, my Saviour, carried me all the way.

We seek love in this, our fading home,
But restless within, from heart to heart we roam.
Searching for something, that will remain forever new,
Searching for something, that will remain forever true.
And hard it is, for us, faithful love to find,
Disappointed, we harden our hearts and mind.
And while I weep with broken heart,
He holds my hand, precious to him, he set me apart.

O beloved Friend, I cannot leave his hand,
He who, from the miry clay,
On a rock, made me stand.
When my steps were a weary,
And the world from me did stray,
O beloved Friend ! He, my Saviour, carried me all the way.

O Brother, Sister, Beloved Friend,
This my Saviour, now and to the end.
His precious hand, I cannot leave,
To his cross, I shall always cleave.
For he loved me, when I was sinner, and not saint,
Clothed in his righteousness, his blood, now my paint.
From sin to glory, He has called me,
this now, my only story.

O Brother, Sister, Beloved Friend,
I cannot leave his precious hand,
But won't you come and stand with me?
There's room, on this rock, you'll see.
I pray, you would seek his holy face,
Come to know, his abiding grace.
O Brother, Sister, Beloved Friend,
May you find in Christ, your only end.

Our God

Yahweh is such a fascinating God. The more I read the Bible, the more I fall in love with the God of the Bible. The plan of salvation is such an incredible one. God the Father, in his love, created and brought to pass, a plan that would save us, once for all, from the jaws of hell and fit us for heaven. We did nothing and can do nothing, to contribute to this plan. It was made long before our existence and brought to pass too, long before our existence and yet because of that plan and his saving grace, we no longer have to fear sin or hell; we have a home in heaven for sure. What else could describe love, more than this plan? It was not just a plan; the execution of this plan meant, the Son of God would need to come to earth, bear our sin and then die for it, to buy our pardon. God the Father loved his Son from eternity past, long before anything came into existence and yet for our (sinners) sake, he sent his beloved Son, to die on a cross, to pay the price of our sin and bridge once and for all, the gap between God and man. Because of Christ's death on the cross and his intercession on our behalf, we can approach the throne of God boldly, because we know our sinful selves are now clothed in the righteousness of Christ. In the light of all that he has done for us, what have we to fear? What can friend or foe, do to us? And yet so foolishly sometimes, we launch into worry and fear, because of circumstances around us; we forget that Yahweh is greater than anyone we know! He did the impossible for us even when we didn't ask him! If he cared for us, even before we came into existence, do we really need to worry if he is watching over us now? Of course he is! No circumstance, however great or small, deserves our worry. Our God watches! He is just, fair, loving, and comforting! He is more than we will ever need. He promises that he watches over us! He offers rest to those who will come to him; He freely gives his peace. We have nothing to fear!

John 3: 16-18

"For God so loved the world, that he gave his only Son, that whoever believes in him should not perish but have eternal life. For God did not send his Son into the world to condemn the world, but in order that the world might be saved through him. Whoever believes in him is not condemned, but whoever does not believe is condemned already, because he has not believed in the name of the only Son of God."

2 Corinthians 5:18-21

All this is from God, who through Christ reconciled us to himself and gave us the ministry of reconciliation; that is, in Christ God was reconciling the world to himself, not counting their trespasses against them, and entrusting to us the message of reconciliation. Therefore, we are ambassadors for Christ, God making his appeal through us. We implore you on behalf of Christ, be reconciled to God. For our sake, he made him to be sin who knew no sin, so that in him we might become the righteousness of God.

Psalm 121:4

Behold, he who keeps Israel will neither slumber nor sleep.

There's a God

There's a God who watches over,
The meek, the weak, the humble, the poor.
He hears, he sees, he never sleeps,
Those stayed upon him.
In perfect peace, he keeps.

There's a God who always works.
The good, the bad, the difficult.
And every ugliness that lurks,
Into perfect good, for all who have belief.
In Him, all men shall find rest and relief.

There's a God who offers pardon.
For sinners who need to be forgiven,
He loves, like no Father ever could,
He gives, like no Father ever would.
He is the judge and yet offers the sacrificial plea.

There's a God who is like no other,
He is love, wrath, justice, and peace!
He's a friend to all who are in need,
He is the saviour, to those sinners, who plead.
He heals, he restores, and fits us for heaven evermore.

Learning All is His

I have had the privilege of growing up in a home where the Bible was read, taught, and we were encouraged to memorise scripture. I have also been blessed to attend churches that taught the truth of the Bible without any apology. I am so glad for all of it because even despite having all that knowledge and teaching, it fell short, the day we lost Ava. Knowing Ava was in heaven didn't rid my heart of pain or ache; it didn't make it easier. Knowing Ava was enjoying the gift of eternity, didn't help me be joyful. Knowing Ava was in the presence of Christ's glory, didn't make me want to give up my sorrow. Knowing Ava would never feel pain, ache, or sin didn't make me cry tears of joy; quite the contrary, actually. I also felt terribly guilty and wondered, was I being punished for saying "Mine"? Context, I love kids, and I'm not sure how to bring that out in words because you probably have to see me with them to understand. I absolutely adore and enjoy the company of little humans. In all honesty, I've not always been sure of "marriage," but without having to take the time to think, I'd say "yes" to "motherhood" anytime, and every time. But here I am, single and probably clock all ticked out on motherhood, so this niece or nephew, would definitely have been someone I loved more than anything else in this world. Also, a fallout with someone close robbed me of years with kids I considered my own, so this gift of niece or nephew, was a fulfilment of so much more for me! And friends too would tell me, "Finally, one that's YOURS!" And I dared to use the word "Mine" often in reference to the baby.

So I wondered, if God was teaching me a lesson, because I may have aroused his jealousy. I do not know why God took Ava away, but I do know everything he does, works out for the good of those who love Him. Scripture flooded my heart and made me realise, All things belong to him. Ava was not mine; she was his, long before I even knew of her existence. Colossians worked as a good reminder. All things are created by him and for him, even Ava, my Ava, our Ava. Job too was another reminder, *The Lord giveth and the Lord taketh away, blessed be the name of the Lord!* I remembered Isaiah and *the people I formed for my pleasure* bit. Everything is his; He creates and brings into existence whatever there is! Ava is his, just like I am too. Again, I have to confess, the knowledge of "*All is His*" doesn't make it easy to accept, that He gets to take away, what's his, even harder to accept, Ava was his to give, and his to take. I can't say I've learnt the lesson, but this I can testify, I am learning and it is painful.

Isaiah 45:12
"I made the earth
and created man on it."

Colossians 1:16
For by him, all things were created, in heaven and on earth, visible and invisible, whether thrones or dominions or rulers or authorities—all things were created through him and for him.

Ava

Ava, my darling niece.
To have and to hold is a dream I may never know,
But a niece or a nephew, that would have been my glow.
I'd love them as if, they were my very own,
I'd do everything for them, shield them from any mourn.
Through them, I'd learn what motherhood could have been,
Through them, I'd learn what adoption would mean!
My niece or nephew would have been my treasure.
Being their Athai (Aunt), would have been, my daily pleasure.
Their inception alone, made me feel possessive and proud,
Mine, I said, like that was a decision I was allowed.
But in time, God broke and humbled my heart.
Showed me, my niece, he had set apart!
Called her to be his and his alone,
Not mine, simply to us on loan!
Now to him, Ava, forever belongs,
My heart weeps, as for Ava I long.
I see her brave, loving, kind, Mom and Dad.
And I wish she were here, to make them glad.
I wish her grandparents, could hold her tight,
Her uncle and aunties, tell her stories at night.
Oft, my heart floods with anger and despair,
Yet I still know, that Ava rests, in his precious care.
Mine, she never was, simply his,
We were all allowed, just a hug, hold and kiss.

Ava reminded me, all things were created through him and for him,
Ava, knit together in her mother's womb, but held together by him.
Even with this knowledge, tears stream down my face,
But one day, I'll laugh with Ava beside, at his throne of grace.

Tranquillity

I was 23 and living in Hungary. I spoke only English and most of them only spoke Magyar, which is Hungarian. But God in his kindness, led me to Golgota, Eger. I had a good job that kept me very busy and then a series of unpleasant, unfair, unjust things happened at work and one day, I woke up to find myself without a job. I didn't have savings or anyone else to see me through this phase, and I didn't want to worry anyone back home, but was I worried? Of course I was. A million thoughts ran through my head, my bank balance flashed before my eyes, I was suddenly aware of every forint (Hungarian currency) I spent. I immediately started calculating how long it would take me to get my things in order while I still had the money, to bring myself back home safely. But even as I worried about all this, scripture started flooding my heart and mind. Psalms, Isaiah, Matthew. I remembered a sermon where the preacher introduced the first line of Psalm 23 as "The Lord is my shepherd; I shall have no need of want". Then that great hymn of old, I recalled "Be still my soul". I called my pastor in Hungary and another good friend, and they both reminded me to do the same – Be still! I took my worry to the Lord and indeed, he answered with rest in the midst of this trial. It wasn't long before my pastor and friend helped me secure interviews, and within just a few days, I had two offers. God provided! I went on to spend that year in Hungary and oh! more trials came my way, He still provided rest!

Psalm 91:9-10
Because you have made the Lord your dwelling place—
the Most High, who is my refuge,
no evil shall be allowed to befall you,
No plague come near your tent.

Psalm 121:2-3
My help comes from the Lord,
who made heaven and earth.
He will not let your foot be moved;
He who keeps you will not slumber.

Isaiah 43:2
When you pass through the waters, I will be with you;
and through the rivers, they shall not overwhelm you;
when you walk through fire you shall not be burned,
and the flame shall not consume you.

Matthew 6:25
"Therefore I tell you, do not be anxious about your life, what you
will eat or what you will drink, nor about your body, what you
will put on. Is not life more than food, and the body more than
clothing?"

James 1:2-3
Count it all joy, my brothers, when you meet trials of various kinds,
for you know that the testing of your faith produces steadfastness.

Be Still My Soul!

Be still my soul,
Thy Lord liveth.
He heareth thy unspoken word,
He calmeth thy waning spirit.

Be still my soul,
Thy Lord reigneth,
He giveth comfort to the weak.
He holdeth dear the weary.

Be still my soul,
Thy Lord is enthroned,
No foe can harm thee,
No flame, scorch thee.

Be still my soul,
Thy Lord speaketh,
In the midst of odd quietness,
His healing voice abideth.

Be still my soul,
Thy Lord loves,
Thy rest, in his loving arms,
Thy joy, in his abiding grace.

Be still my soul,
Thy Lord is Lord,
He unsharpeneth every sword,
He fighteth thine every battle.

Be still my soul,
Thy Lord knoweth,
Thine trials, his work of art, in thee,
Thine endurance, his reflection of glory, in thee.

Be still my soul,
Thy Lord is Shepherd,
Thou art truly his,
Thine pastures ever green. Amen

Sinner to Saint

Dust to glory, rags to riches, these are all fascinating stories, but nothing is as fascinating, as sinner to saint. Such was the story of Apostle Paul. What a beginning and what an end! Paul has to be one of the most intriguing discoveries in the New Testament as you read through it. It is amazing to see the transformation Christ brings about in a sinner. You learn, that Paul was full of righteous Jewish zeal, to persecute Christians, and then you learn, God chooses this vile, terrible, murderous-Christian-killing Jew, to take his gospel, to the Gentiles! This Paul, who once orchestrated the stoning of a saintly man, Stephen, became an apostle, who planted churches. Today, Paul's legacy, is the churches he planted across Asia Minor and Greece. Paul is the best encouragement any sinner could ever want. He is the testament, that God can work with the worst, and make the best. Take courage, sinners. If God could work in Paul, in such an awe-inspiring way, He can do the same with us. What then do we do to be a Paul and not a Saul? Follow what Paul did! The account of Paul's conversion tells us, he heard the voice, he answered it, he obeyed it. That's all it took, to make a Saul into a Paul. And this same Paul, ah! What a life he lived. He had the audacity to say "Follow me". Many of us Christians love preaching Christ to others, but we also very quickly like to tell them "Don't follow me, follow Christ" and we say that not out of humility, but because we are giving ourselves room to sin. We have an excuse to say "I'm just a man" but not Paul! He said "Follow me". Paul walked so closely with Christ, he knew his life emulated Christ and so there was no danger in saying "Follow me". What a lesson for us all, to walk the talk! May we, like Paul, have only room for Christ in our life! May we become bold enough to say to sinners, Follow me! And may that following of us, lead them to Christ! And while we draw encouragement from Paul's story, let's not forget that he suffered for the sake of the gospel! Paul didn't just preach Christ, he lived Christ! His life really is a lesson that teaches us, to count everything else as loss, and only seek Christ, for he alone is gain. May we, like Paul, find contentment, in Christ alone.

Acts 9:7-22

So Ananias departed and entered the house. And laying his hands on him, he said, "Brother Saul, the Lord Jesus who appeared to you on the road by which you came has sent me so that you may regain your sight and be filled with the Holy Spirit." And immediately something like scales fell from his eyes, and he regained his sight. Then he rose and was baptised; and taking food, he was strengthened. For some days he was with the disciples at Damascus. And immediately he proclaimed Jesus in the synagogues, saying, "He is the Son of God." And all who heard him were amazed and said, "Is not this the man who made havoc in Jerusalem of those who called upon this name? And has he not come here for this purpose, to bring them bound before the chief priests?" But Saul increased all the more in strength, and confounded the Jews who lived in Damascus by proving that Jesus was the Christ.

Paul

Have you heard about the man named Paul?
Who was obedient and true, to his summon and call?

A man of faith and an apostle, indeed, was he,
For our dear Lord, in him, a faithful servant did see.

Saul, a fervent Jew, didn't live for our Lord,
At first, he spent his life persecuting our God.

Despite his vile behaviour and ugly zeal,
The Lord chose him, before him, to kneel.

Paul went on his way to Damascus, Christians to jail,
But instead God met him halfway, his plan to fail.

On his way to Damascus, from heaven, great light did he see,
And he heard our dear Lord say, "Why dost thou persecute me?"

On hearing the great voice, he realised, God it was,
That moment, struck by blindness, his life came to a pause.

Obedient to the voice, he did what it said,
He rushed to Ananias, who laid hands on his head.

Ananias revealed to Saul the plans of our God,
He told him, he would now be an instrument, for the Lord.

That day, with sight, was born a new man in Saul,
Now, to the new world, better known as Paul.

His mission, no longer, Christians to kill,
His only mission now, Gentiles with Christ, to fill.

He stayed true to his calling, right to the very end,
No shipwreck, no flogging, could make his mind bend.

Thus in vile Saul, was born the great Apostle Paul,
Amongst men of faith, even today he stands tall.

Faith-Full?

Hebrews is one of my favourite books in the Bible. I love how the author begins the book itself. I love how he brings out who Jesus is and all the comparisons he makes, to let us know Jesus is more superior than any other being and yet identical in nature and essence, to God the Father. One of my favourite chapters in Hebrews has to be Chapter 11. It lists some of the men I truly admire most. I learnt about all these men as bedtime stories from my Dad, so they have always been precious. Chapter 11 begins with the definition of what faith is and then goes on to list those men and women, who had great faith in the Old and New Testament. Every person mentioned in Chapter 11, is worthy of individual study, because they lived out what faith is supposed to be! They all lived their faith with gusto; it was evident in their choices and lives. I often wonder if I could have ever had faith like them, in those times. I find myself failing at faith, even now, with the written Bible in my hands, and those men and women mentioned in Chapter 11 didn't even have that with them. Abraham obeyed just by hearing God, and he left familiar surroundings, to be an alien in a foreign land! Moses, chose to be mistreated, rather than enjoy the riches of Pharaoh's palace. By faith, the Israelites crossed the Red Sea, and it was faith that saved Rahab from doom. There's more written about plenty of others, but the commonality between them all, remains faith! They all had faith in Yahweh and Jesus, and they knew, it was only through unwavering faith that they could please God. They were not only aware, that this wasn't their home, they lived with the conviction of it. They eagerly awaited that country that was promised to them! The faith mentioned in Hebrews 11 isn't unnatural; it actually is a faith that we each, can claim for ourselves.

Hebrews 1:3-5
He is the radiance of the glory of God and the exact imprint of his nature, and he upholds the universe by the word of his power. After making purification for sins, he sat down at the right hand of the Majesty on high, having become as much superior to angels as the name he has inherited is more excellent than theirs.
Hebrews 11:1
Now faith is the assurance of things hoped for, the conviction of things not seen.

Hebrews 11:6
And without faith, it is impossible to please him, for whoever would draw near to God must believe that he exists and that he rewards those who seek him.

Hebrews 11:13
These all died in faith, not having received the things promised, but having seen them and greeted them from afar, and having acknowledged that they were strangers and exiles on the earth.

Hebrews 11:39-40
And all these, though commended through their faith, did not receive what was promised. Since God had provided something better for us, that apart from us they should not be made perfect.

Faith

Have we faith? we each must ask!
Is it real or just our "Christian" mask?
Have we been tried and tested?
Will we with the saints, be found, rested?
For if our faith be in Christ, rooted and true,
We must for trials, ask more, not few!

Abel, his gift, better than Cain,
His sacrifice, counted as righteous and hence faith, his gain.
Enoch, he lived and never saw death,
For his faith, simply taken up, in a breath.
Noah blessed, while God regretted creating man,
His faith found favour, God revealed to him his plan!

Abraham, the great Father of all,
From home, to a foreign land, he obeyed the call!
Never building house, he simply lived in a tent,
Knowing full well, the city whose architect was God, was his
covenant.

Sarah, though old, had the power to conceive,
For she knew he was faithful and his promises, did receive.
Sarah was barren and Abraham as good as dead,
Yet God blessed them, not just with offspring, but nations
instead.

Such faith has been eternally commended,
for they all died, before receiving what was promised!
This world was no home to them, their faith, told the story,
They desired a heavenly one, their only home, one in glory.
For this reason, God isn't ashamed, to be their God,
Because no possession or being, above him, did they laud.
For them, indeed, a special city he has made,
Laid their foundation and given them a citizenship, that will
never fade.
Is such faith easy, you must wonder and ask?
The Bible teaches, though rewarding, it is a difficult task.

From Abraham was asked, what he loved most,
To sacrifice Isaac, the only son, of whom he could boast.
Though promised nations, he had but one son,
And now he was asked to offer a sacrifice, of this one.
But Abraham he believed, Yahweh could do more,
Raise Isaac from the dead, to live evermore.
Such was the faith, of our Father of old,
Refined through scorching fire, his story forever told.

Moses, another great hero of old,
Chose slavery over Egypt's treasures untold.
Born to a Hebrew, by Pharaoh's edict, should have died,
Instead, he wined and dined at Pharaoh's side.
A Hebrew, at home, in Pharaoh's palace,
but chose to roam the wilderness, in Israel's service.
He considered the reproach of Christ, far more worthy,
Than Pharaoh's wealth, which was simply worldly.
From rags to riches, should have been his story,
But embracing poverty and slavery, now his glory.

From slavery to freedom, the Israelites, he led fearlessly,
Marching onward, knowing his reward, he would receive,
eternally.

Isaac, Jacob, Joseph, Rahab, Gideon, Samuel,
Barak, Samson, Jephthah, David, Daniel,
And so many more, have their story of faith told,
In this great book, the Bible, we now hold.
For faith exhibited, they have been commended,
That we follow in their steps, is highly recommended!

Without faith, we can never please God,
Those who believe and seek him, he will reward.
It is by faith we understand, the universe as God's creation,
From nothing to something, he made all things, in every nation.
Our faith ought to be, like the Hebrew fathers, of old,
Who were persecuted and yet found, pure as gold!
To them, faith was more than a mere, sweet sounding word,
To them, faith was the assurance of things hoped for, unseen and
only heard.
And why should we follow, an old, old story?
So that, brothers and sisters, we can live a life of, dust to glory!

Appearance

We live in a world that pays so much attention to appearance. The cosmetic industry is a billion-dollar industry that only steadily grows in economy. From colour, to shape, to height, to weight, we are told what we ought to be, to be beautiful or handsome. Everything is a study! And most of us, conform to this obnoxious demand of society. As a kid, one of the verses I quickly memorised and that became a favourite was, "Man looks at the outward appearance but the Lord looks at the heart". While that's definitely telling us not to work on beautifying our outward appearance, it is also telling us something else: beautify your heart! God looks at our heart and we know there are plenty of verses in the Bible that tell us how terribly horrible our heart is, so clearly beauty in the heart is not natural, we need to work at it. As Christians, our beauty is seen in the likeness of Christ. The more Christlike we become, the more beauty will be seen in us.

1 Samuel 16:7
But the Lord said to Samuel,"Do not look on his appearance or on the height of his stature, because I have rejected him. For the Lord sees not as man sees: man looks on the outward appearance, but the Lord looks on the heart."

Colossians 3:12-14
Put on then, as God's chosen ones, holy and beloved, compassionate hearts, kindness, humility, meekness, and patience, bearing with

one another and, if one has a complaint against another, forgiving each other; as the Lord has forgiven you, so you also must forgive. And above all these put on love, which binds everything together in perfect harmony.

Galatians 5:22-25
But the fruit of the Spirit is love, joy, peace, patience, kindness, goodness, faithfulness, gentleness, self-control; against such things there is no law. And those who belong to Christ Jesus have crucified the flesh with its passions and desires. If we live by the Spirit, let us also keep in step with the Spirit. Let us not become conceited, provoking one another, envying one another.

Ephesians 4:22-24
To put off your old self, which belongs to your former manner of life and is corrupt through deceitful desires, and to be renewed in the spirit of your minds, and to put on the new self, created after the likeness of God in true righteousness and holiness.

Reflection

By the waters, away from the world, I stand alone,
Suddenly aware of a liquid clone.
I look at my reflection, but my smile grows faint.
Stands there a woman, coloured in wretched paint.
That woman's beauty so horribly feign,
That woman's beauty, no beauty to gain.

By the waters, I stoop, carefully to see,
That woman who looks so much like me.
I see there, no beauty, anyone would adorn,
I see there an ugliness, like I have never known.
I stand alone, consumed in my great sorrow,
This horrid face that will define my tomorrow.
I fall on my knees and let out a helpless sigh.
What have I become? My loud, anxious cry.

By the waters, I sit, desperate to change the reflection,
A task impossible, despite the stream's deflection.
There is One, who clothes with righteousness, I had long ago
learnt,
Who beauty to adorn me, on a horrid cross, did earn.
So I say a prayer to that Holy One above,
Asking to be clothed, in his rich, cleansing love,
To be adorned with the beauty, He freely gives,
For I hear, only he, truly forgives.

By the waters, I now rest, in calm and peace,
Content in his love and grace, that I know shall never cease.
I look into the waters now running wild,
I see there a sinner, now embraced, as precious child.
Amazed, I watch how the ugliness fades,
Until all there is, is a reflection of me, as with grace, He bathes.
I see there in the water, a sight I can now begin to love,
I see there a sinner, drenched in righteousness, flowing from
Christ above.

Wretched Sinner

Do you sometimes feel like it is impossible for a certain someone to be saved? You might be thinking, "Oh goodness, this person is so terrible, not even Jesus can save him or her!" The truth is, God can save the vilest of sinners. In the midst of the crucifixion and its horrifying, glorious account, is a story I hold very dear: the dying thief! He is such a splendid example of a vile sinner being saved. If "Nick in time" were personified, it would be this dying thief. He wasn't someone who did good, he wasn't someone who others liked, he wasn't someone of great honour; instead, he was a thief, someone the people wanted punished, someone who deserved a death on a cross. Besides his sin against the people, he mocked Christ too, while he hung on that cross – the audacity, right? Yet as the hours went by, something changed for this dying thief, something that caused him now to believe in Christ as Saviour. He exercised similar faith like Shadrach, Meshach, and Abednego; he was able to recognise that Christ had the power to save him from a grave situation. Luke has it recorded for us. Imagine the fate of this thief when he woke up that morning; he must have been full of doom, he knew the punishment that awaited him, he had nothing to look forward to, except death, and then he believes in Christ and suddenly, death was not his end; eternity with Christ would now be his end. Talk about a last-minute save – what grace!

William Cowper's "There is a fountain" also tells of this amazing grace that the dying thief received.

Matthew 27:44

And the robbers who were crucified with him also reviled him in the same way.

Mark 15:32

Those who were crucified with him also reviled him.

Luke 23:39-43

One of the criminals who was hanged railed at him, saying, "Are you not the Christ? Save yourself and us!" But the other rebuked him, saying, "Do you not fear God, since you are under the same sentence of condemnation? And we indeed justly, for we are receiving the due reward of our deeds; but this man has done nothing wrong." And he said, "Jesus, remember me when you come into your kingdom." And he said to him," Truly, I say to you, today you will be with me in paradise."

Isaiah 50:2

Is my hand shortened, that it cannot redeem?

The Dying Thief

He knew his hour was very near.
Soon he'd be far from everything dear.
It was to be the most dreadful day of his life,
He was to pay for the deeds, of his hands and knife.
He always did know very well,
His sins, would finally lead to hell.
So indeed, today was that fateful day.
When his soul would be cast away.
Not a soul would indeed care to pray,
They wanted revenge, for all he claimed as "prey."
So people prepared to cheer his death,
He decided to stay strong, until his very last breath.
He was soon brought, to that cruel tree,
Where he'd be nailed for everyone to see.
An open spectacle for one and all,
The day justice on him, would eternally befall.
He wasn't alone with his cruel cross,
Two others were sharing, a similar cross.
He looked at them and brightly grinned,
Two of them had indeed, terribly sinned.
But the other man, who they called "Christ",
He knew, was pure, yet utterly despised.
Both he and his other sinful friend,
This Christ, with mockery, did befriend.
They both loathed and reviled him,

But he didn't respond, until the hour was dim.
This thief, who "the Christ" had mocked,
Understood "grace" as the hours clocked.
He began to revere, the man on his side,
And recognized, that holiness was beside.
No longer was he part, of the other thief's mock,
No longer did he think "Christ" worth a laughing stock.
The dying thief had received "grace,"
He soon addressed that crucified face,
"Lord, remember me in heaven," I pray,
Christ assured him, he would soon, in paradise stay.
That thief, though sinful, died blessed,
For what waited for him was eternal rest.
He knew his heart would not be sinful, for long.
For he now to Christ, would eternally belong.
That grace which touched the dying thief,
Is given to all who will, in Christ, find belief.
If that dying thief found amazing grace,
There is hope, for every single race.
Like the thief, if we recognise sin,
We can repent and let Christ dwell in.
That thief's life, was vile indeed,
But his death, a lesson we all did need.

Wholehearted Follower

I've read Corinthians even as a child, but the time it stung me, was when we were going through the book of Romans, at church and my pastor referred to *"Examine yourselves, to see whether you are in the faith. Test yourselves. Or do you not realise this about yourselves, that Jesus Christ is in you? —unless indeed you fail to meet the test!"* It really made me want to examine and be sure. I recalled Matthew where it says *"Not everyone who says to me, 'Lord, Lord,' will enter the kingdom of heaven, but the one who does the will of my Father who is in heaven."* That's a scary thought, isn't it, to imagine you are saved but you really aren't? And then came the series on the kings of the Old Testament. It was so heart-breaking to see, so much sin! So many were chosen over God's appointed people, but were leading them astray, rather than to God. Even though some began well, they had a terrible ending. It made me realise I need to be examining myself regularly. Am I really in the faith? Am I doing what Jesus would want me to do? While there are plenty of examples of those who fell away – the kings, Israelites etc. I am grateful for Moses in the Old Testament (among others) and Paul in the New Testament, who are proof that you can run the race for the Lord, fervently, to the end. They give me hope that my race can end well too. From them, I've learnt the key to remaining faithful, is to ensure, that I am abiding in God, and to abide in God, I need to abide in his word.

2 Kings 17:9

And the people of Israel did secretly against the Lord their God things that were not right. They built for themselves high places in all their towns, from watchtower to fortified city.

2 Kings 17:13

Yet the Lord warned Israel and Judah by every prophet and every seer, saying, "Turn from your evil ways and keep my commandments and my statutes, in accordance with all the law that I commanded your fathers, and that I sent to you by my servants the prophets."

2 Kings 17:18

Therefore, the Lord was very angry with Israel and removed them out of his sight. None was left but the tribe of Judah only.

John 15:1-6

I am the true vine, and my Father is the vinedresser. Every branch in me that does not bear fruit he takes away, and every branch that does bear fruit he prunes, that it may bear more fruit. Already you are clean because of the word that I have spoken to you. Abide in me, and I in you. As the branch cannot bear fruit by itself, unless it abides in the vine, neither can you, unless you abide in me. I am the vine; you are the branches. Whoever abides in me and I in him, he it is that bears much fruit, for apart from me you can do nothing. If anyone does not abide in me he is thrown away like a branch and withers; and the branches are gathered, thrown into the fire, and burned.

My Heart's Cry

From the depths of my heart, O Father, I cry,
Keep me faithful, keep me humbly serving, until the day I die.
For in history, I see, they embraced your word,
And yet lived like, your word, they'd never heard.
In vanity, they simply spent their, worthless life,
Forsaking you, when called to bear trial or strife.

From the depths of my heart, O Father, I cry,
Keep me faithful, keep me humbly serving, until the day I die.
For even your blessed," chosen" race,
Who received, grace upon grace,
Didn't seek you, with all their heart,
Failed to acknowledge you, as the God, who set Israel apart.

From the depths of my heart, O Father, I cry
Keep me faithful, keep me humbly serving, until the day I die.
Let me not be, like those many kings,
Who you chose, with love and grace
Who in times of plenty and need,
Only to idols, praises did sing.

From the depths of my heart, O Father, I cry.
Keep me faithful, keep me humbly serving, until the day I die.
Let me be like, that great, prophet of old,
And honour you, like I am told.

That prophet, who chose not, name or riches.
But simply your name, to love and uphold,
And your people, to rescue, from Pharaoh's hold.

From the depths of my heart, O Father, I cry,
Keep me faithful, keep me humbly serving, until the day I die.
Let me, like Paul, run my race,
Let me never for granted, take thy loving grace.
Sin behind me, cross before me,
Let me run swiftly, only to thy throne.

From the depths of my heart, O Father, I cry,
Keep me faithful, keep me humbly serving, until the day I die.
Let me, like Jesus, always do thy will,
May I, like Him, your work on earth fulfil.
And should it be, just his cross I carry,
May I, like him, say, "Your will, not mine, be done."
From the depths of my heart, O Father, I cry,
Keep me faithful, keep me humbly serving, until the day I die.

Our God, the Greatest Artist

Ever felt like your current situation makes absolutely no sense? Ever wondered what God could be doing to work this current, crazy situation, for your good? I have felt like that many a time in my life, like my life makes no sense at all, and it's all just a cruel joke. But I am grateful for my parents, who made me memorise scripture and thus practice, the art of hiding scripture in my heart! Because on days when I want to give up and believe there is no good, the word of God draws me back to him. On days when I feel my life is pointless, God has often used these verses to remind me, He is sovereign and always in control. He is the potter; all I am is the clay. He will make of me something beautiful, in His time. The hardest thing to do often, is wait. But any artist will tell you, patience is what makes their art beautiful. They pour in hours of work, which finally yields beautiful results. God too takes his time with us, sometimes because he wants us to be still, sometimes because we resist his work in us, but no matter the delay or resistance, God will work his beauty in us and that we can be sure of. He has a plan for every single one of us, and He will bring it to completion.

Philippians 1:6
And I am sure of this, that he who began a good work in you will bring it to completion on the day of Jesus Christ.

Romans 8:28-29
And we know that for those who love God, all things work together for good, for those who are called according to his purpose. For those whom he foreknew, he also predestined to be conformed to the image of his Son, in order that he might be the firstborn among many brothers.

Isaiah 43: 1-2
But now thus says the Lord,
he who created you, O Jacob,
He who formed you, O Israel:
"Fear not, for I have redeemed you;
I have called you by name, you are mine.
When you pass through the waters, I will be with you;
and through the rivers, they shall not overwhelm you;
when you walk through fire you shall not be burned,
and the flame shall not consume you.

Jeremiah 18:6
O house of Israel, can I not do with you as this potter has done? declares the Lord. Behold, like the clay in the potter's hand, so are you in my hand, O house of Israel.

The Painter

Upon the canvas blank and white,
Lay my life, as clear as light.
For many a day, thus it lay.
Drenched with water, from colour, away.
So dull the scene, so hopeless, the art,
So void of beauty, so rid of heart.
Yet thus it lay, for all to see,
Among the Painter's most treasured sea.
None could understand the canvas's worth,
None could picture it, as beauty's birth.
Then one day, when the canvas was pale and dry,
The painter drew mighty strokes, low and high.
He worked at it both, day and night,
He captured colours, rare and bright.
And then, he smiled at the finished piece,
At beauty which his paintbrush released.
The canvas, no longer dull or boring,
But the very story, of beauty evolving.
Thus my life, no longer pale or white,
But stroked artistically, with beauty bright.
My Painter's hand, empowered by skill,
He turneth water into wine, by His will.

All Things for Our Good

Romans 8:28 is a favourite of so many and yet, sadly, it's not quite understood. *"And we know that for those who love God all things work together for good, for those who are called according to his purpose."* The "all things" here refers to literally "ALL THINGS" meaning, the things that are terrible, the things that are hard, the things that break our heart, the things that make us sad, the things that hurt us, the things that shake us, ALL THINGS! All these things, though difficult and terrible and beyond our understanding, these things God will work for our good, meaning that promotion we didn't get, that pay cut we just received, that friend we lost, that wedding that didn't happen, that miscarriage, that adoption that fell through, that stillborn baby, all those painfully hard trials, that, He will work, for our good. And what is the good? We need the next verse for it – verse 29 says *"For those whom he foreknew he also predestined to be conformed to the image of his Son, in order that he might be the firstborn among many brothers."* It is hard to imagine that situations we dread or that cause us pain could ever be "good", and the truth is, during the situation, we might never see the good, but we can be sure that he will work it for our good! He is conforming us into the image of his Son! In hindsight, after the passing of that period, we will see the good he worked out for us. But here's the key, the "good" is not for everyone, the "good" is worked out for those who love God and are called to his purposes.

Joseph was a fantastic example of this, how something that seemed terribly bad, worked out for his good. Daniel is another example, too. Both Joseph and Daniel rose from slavery, to being the right hand of Pharaoh, and right hand of king Nebuchadnezzar. These Jewish boys became revered and honoured, in a land that enslaved Jews. Joseph and Daniel's "good" was not just the honour they received from people, or Pharaoh, or the king, but in that glorious Chapter 11 of Hebrews, their faith is made mention of. The "good" they received held eternal value!

Genesis 50: 19-20
But Joseph said to them, "Do not fear, for am I in the place of God? As for you, you meant evil against me, but God meant it for good, to bring it about that many people should be kept alive, as they are today."

Daniel 2:47-48
The king answered and said to Daniel, "Truly, your God is God of gods and Lord of kings, and a revealer of mysteries, for you have been able to reveal this mystery." Then the king gave Daniel high honours and many great gifts, and made him ruler over the whole province of Babylon and chief prefect over all the wise men of Babylon.

Hebrews 11:22
By faith, Joseph, at the end of his life, made mention of the exodus of the Israelites and gave directions concerning his bones.

Hebrews 11:33
who through faith conquered kingdoms, enforced justice, obtained promises, stopped the mouths of lions.

Good

He giveth good things, they said,
She wondered, as her Father
Lay on his deathbed.
Those words, so often she had heard,
T'was something she never tested, never bothered!
But now as he lay silently,
There before her, life fading,
She wondered about those words,
How ridiculous to have ever been uttered!
How can "good" come of this life?
One filled with anger, hatred, and strife?
How could anything ever be good?
This God wasn't worth being understood.
So she buried her Father, sad,
Spent her life, not believing in good, but bad.
Years she spent, in restless vanity,
Suppressing her anger and sorrow,
Trying to keep her sanity!
And when alone, at her Father's graveside,
Hands running through the grass beside,
The fading sun caught her sight, upon the little hill,
With its rich hue, it gave her great joy, and a chill.
Ah! What beauty! she thought, in a sunset,
So rich in its hue, no artist could ever, on paper get.
And there, it dawned upon her, in the midst of this beauty,

The sun came, and the sun went; it did its daily duty.
She gazed upon her Father's grave,
As tears rolled down her tired face.
He came, he left, he did his duty.
Through him, the Lord added to her life, much beauty.
The sun, in all its glory, at rising, was good.
And the sun, in its rich hue, in setting, was good.
She began to understand that all things were good.
Even things that seemed bad, were still meant, for good,
Because He who gave them, was in wisdom, good.
He knows the time and he knows the need,
He giveth things to a man's soul, to feed.
Even in what seems bad, for you, he traces the good,
Even when his children have him, terribly misunderstood.
As she wept upon that grave, God did, again, all for her good.
She was never again broken by bad; in faith, she firmly and
resiliently stood.

Carved

When you see an artist at work, it's quite fascinating, especially one that does sculptures. From a bulky, shabby-looking piece of wood, he carves beauty. On a trip to Sri Lanka, I had the privilege of visiting a wood factory. I marvelled at the colourful masks made there. A 15 year old, took my friend and I around and showed us the logs of wood they used to make these fine pieces of art. The wood was ordinary but the finished piece, extraordinary. The shy 15-year-old, also showed us some of his work, and it was fantastic. This lad sure has a bright future ahead of him, sheer talent was displayed in the pieces he made, at the raw age of fifteen. This lad, though gifted, needed "something" to make his art from. The most impossible and breathtaking art would be, to make "something" from "nothing". The truth is, no one can do that and yet the truth is, that's what God did for us! Thus bringing out yet again why he is God. He is not like man. Genesis tells us the beautiful story of how we came into being according to his will and according to his plan. He created us in his image. There are millions who struggle with this truth, millions who reject it, millions who believe it, and millions who don't want to think about it. But no matter what you think, the Bible tells us, God made "something" from "nothing", and I do not doubt that! From travel, I have learnt, there is beauty in every part of this finely created world. The more beauty I see, the more I'm convinced, man had nothing to do with it; Genesis is simply true. God created all things and it was "Good"! When I look around me, I can't help but marvel at this creator God.

Psalm 19:1

The heavens declare the glory of God, and the sky above proclaims his handiwork.

Romans 1:20

For his invisible attributes, namely, his eternal power and divine nature, have been clearly perceived ever since the creation of the world in the things that have been made. So they are without excuse.

Genesis 1:1-2

In the beginning, God created the heavens and the earth. The earth was without form and void, and darkness was over the face of the deep. And the Spirit of God was hovering over the face of the waters.

Exodus 20:11

For in six days the Lord made heaven and earth, the sea, and all that is in them, and rested on the seventh day. Therefore, the Lord blessed the Sabbath day and made it holy.

Nehemiah 9:6

"You are the Lord, you alone. You have made heaven, the heaven of heavens, with all their host, the earth and all that is on it, the seas and all that is in them; and you preserve all of them; and the host of heaven worships you."

'Tis But Mighty Hands

I know 'tis but mighty hands that carved me,

When I look at the heavens, mountains, and sea.

The heavens, so wide and endless in length,

Reminds me of my Saviour's great strength.

The mountains so lofty, mighty, and bold,

Proves the majesty of my creator God of old.

The sea so vast, deep, and infinitely blue,

Only assure me, of God's existence; I need no other clue.

For how else could any of this come into being,

If it were not the work of him who had no beginning?

I know 'tis but mighty hands that carved me,

When I look at the heavens, mountains, and sea.

I Surrender

"All to Jesus, I surrender; All to Him I freely give; I will ever love and trust Him, In His presence daily live. I surrender all, I surrender all, all to Thee, my blessed Saviour, I surrender all." These lyrics by Judson W. Van DeVenter has been belted out aloud, in many Sunday masses. Personally, I have too, but singing it is easy; living it is mighty hard. Surrendering everything at the feet of Jesus begins with self. I know I fail at it profusely. Even my noblest of thoughts are honestly wrapped in pride and self. When I think of surrender and laying what's precious at the throne of God, there are two Bible characters that come to mind: Moses and Paul. I never cease to be awestruck by Moses and his choice of leading Israel rather than lying in the luxury of Pharaoh's home. To me, that is true surrender, not just the renouncing of name and wealth, but the embrace of poverty and difficulty, on account of God's work. As Christians, it's two asks of us: 1) to consider Christ gain 2) to count everything else, as loss. Both, are essential, for us to truly live a life that pleases God. We see that in Paul too. If there was anyone worthy of praise, it was Paul, for all his accomplishments, and yet he said, "I count it all loss," and he didn't merely say it; you see it in his life. He suffered for the sake of the gospel. We are all called to have the same attitude, to be able to give up everything except Christ and to never forget, our God is a jealous God; he desires to be the one, that we love the most!

Hebrews 11:24-26

By faith, Moses, when he was grown up, refused to be called the son of Pharaoh's daughter, choosing rather to be mistreated with the people of God than to enjoy the fleeting pleasures of sin. He considered the reproach of Christ greater wealth than the treasures of Egypt, for he was looking to the reward.

Philippians 3:8-9

Indeed, I count everything as loss because of the surpassing worth of knowing Christ Jesus my Lord. For his sake, I have suffered the loss of all things and count them as rubbish, in order that I may gain Christ and be found in him, not having a righteousness of my own that comes from the law, but that which comes through faith in Christ, the righteousness from God that depends on faith.

Mark 12:29-30

Jesus answered, "The most important thing is, 'Hear, O Israel: The Lord our God, the Lord is one. And you shall love the Lord your God with all your heart and with all your soul and with all your mind and with all your strength.'"

Exodus 20:3

You shall have no other gods before me.

Take it All Away

Take it all away, Oh! Just take it all away,
Everything I own, everything on display.
Strip me bare, keep me naked,
Keep me forever, in Christ awakened.

Take it all away, Oh! Just take it all away,
My family, my friends, keep them at bay.
Let me count it all, but mere loss,
Let me cling, to your cleansing cross.

Take it all away, Oh! Just take it all away,
My hopes, my desires, my will, and way.
Let me lose sight, of all earthly things,
Keep me focused on Christ, and the joy He brings.

Take it all away, Oh! Just take it all away,
All worldly pleasures, that cause me to sway.
Let me run swiftly, the race that's laid out,
Let me not be distracted, by random things about.

Take it all away, Oh! Just take it all away,
My sin, my might, my selfish play.
Keep me living, only for Christ's glory,
Keep me alive, to tell salvation's story.

Take it all away, Oh! Just take it all away,
Only keep me longing, for my home far away.
Never let me roam, never let me stray.
Keep me forever in your fold; this I pray.

Heavenly Abode

I've thought of heaven often but ever so much, since Ava made it her home. I have wondered and been a tad bit haunted by it too. I know, because the Bible tells me, that Christ will be the main attraction in heaven. It's not the pearly gates or gem-laden road that's going to have me excited, it is Christ but I am also excited about those who I knew, who I will see again, or is *"In the sweet by and by, we shall meet on that beautiful shore"* only lyrics to a lovely hymn? We believe as Christians that we do not need to grieve death, for those who are in Christ Jesus, because eternity awaits them, that died, and eternity awaits us, the living. So then, shouldn't that mean we will know each other in heaven? I firmly believe we will. Based on 1 Thessalonians and its comfort, I believe we will recognise those whom we know here on earth, when we are in heaven. The story of the rich man, Lazarus, and Abraham is yet another reason I believe there will be recognition in heaven. Luke 10 talks about our names being written in heaven, indicating individuality, and I'm sure that must mean we have unique identity even in heaven. Also, Moses and Elijah appeared at the transfiguration, and Peter recognised them, that must mean people can be identified as who they were, here on earth. Since Ava left, that's something I have thought about a lot, recognising the ones I love, who were in Christ Jesus. For some time, I was of the opinion, yes, we'd recognise others, but we actually wouldn't be near anyone but Jesus. But as I studied the word and thought about it more, heaven is described as a home, made up of family.

The essence of family is loving one another. That made me think, in a family, we greet and meet everyone, we know everyone, if heaven is one big family, I will know my Dad and Ava once again in heaven. I will get to enjoy their company along with the saints I've admired in the Bible, in the presence of Christ's unwavering glory, what a delight that's going to be!

Ephesians 3:15

"from whom every family in heaven and on earth is named."

1 Thessalonians 4:13-18

But we do not want you to be uninformed, brothers, about those who are asleep, that you may not grieve as others do who have no hope. For since we believe that Jesus died and rose again, even so, through Jesus, God will bring with him those who have fallen asleep. For this, we declare to you by a word from the Lord, that we who are alive, who are left until the coming of the Lord, will not precede those who have fallen asleep. For the Lord himself will descend from heaven with a cry of command, with the voice of an archangel, and with the sound of the trumpet of God. And the dead in Christ will rise first. Then we who are alive, who are left, will be caught up together with them in the clouds to meet the Lord in the air, and so we will always be with the Lord. Therefore, encourage one another with these words.

I Wonder

I wonder what you did up there,
while we laid you in the ground?
I wonder if you were sleeping, crawling.
Or just running around?
I wonder if you look at us and think,
Ah! They know grief like I never will,
Or if you simply smile and think,
How much can they cry, still?
I wonder if Earth
Could have ever been, as pleasant, as your heavenly home is?
I wonder if Heaven
Could ever be dull, or void of sufficient bliss?
I wonder how you spend your time,
cause ours seems to have come to a standstill,
I wonder when our hearts will be calmed,
Simply knowing, it was God's will.
I wonder and wonder,
all the time,
Cause Ava, I wish you were here,
But one day we'll wander.
in our heavenly home
And Ava, you will be forever near!

Pistis

"*Pistis*" is the Greek word for "faith." It appears more than 240 times in the New Testament alone. The word is used to express "confidence in Christ." Every Christian is called to have faith like that, which has confidence in Christ. And such faith is what we have, because of what Christ did on the cross. Once for all, he saved man from himself, and the consequences of sin. It is because of Christ's finished work at Calvary, that those who believe in Christ Jesus, will no longer face damnation but have crossed over, from death to life. Now, this faith is not something we hide; this faith is what we profess, day in and day out, to everyone we meet. We have the good news that brings life, my friend. We are called to take this news to the ends of the earth. Hope is alive because of such faith, and it is our duty, to bring hope and faith, to the lost souls we encounter. And while we have a duty to the unsaved, we have a duty to the saved too. We are called to spur our fellow brothers and sisters in the church. The church is where we fuel our walk with Christ; it's the place that reminds us, who Christ is and what he's done for us, because everyone in the church has nothing to boast about, save from the fact that, by grace, they have been saved through Christ Jesus. The church ought to be the place where love and good works never cease, because Christ is alive there, and we Christians are called to imitate him. Christ left us an example; he served his people until his very last breath. We are called to serve like him, and we are called to serve in our local church; this is what is pleasing to God.

Ephesians 2:8
For by grace, you have been saved through faith.

Hebrews 9:12-14
He entered once for all into the holy places, not by means of the blood of goats and calves but by means of his own blood, thus securing an eternal redemption. For if the blood of goats and bulls, and the sprinkling of defiled persons with the ashes of a heifer, sanctify for the purification of the flesh, how much more will the blood of Christ, who through the eternal Spirit offered himself without blemish to God, purify our conscience from dead works to serve the living God.

John 5:24
Truly, truly, I say to you, whoever hears my word and believes in him who sent me has eternal life. He does not come into judgement, but has passed from death to life.

Matthew 20:28
Even as the Son of Man came not to be served but to serve, and to give his life as a ransom for many.

Faith and Hope

Oh! For sinners, such a home,
In God's house, there's room; no more we roam.
Our confidence, in Christ alone,
Washed in his blood, we are his own.

Chorus
This the story, Christ, our glory,
Sought by grace, Bought by blood,
The Redeemed, we are one,
Oh! Praise to the Father, Spirit, Son.

Now draw we near, to our dear Lord,
Hearts filled with faith, in our good God.
Conscience cleansed, minds restored,
May his will, in our lives, be enthroned.

Now hold we fast, to the hope we know,
To our brothers and sisters, this hope, we show.
Faithful is he, who has promised us more,
His sacrifice has torn the curtain, opened the door.

Now to the church, his beloved bride,
In him alone, we boast and pride.
Spurred by him, we spur one another,
With love and good works, we bless each other.

Golgotha

My church in Hungary was called "Golgota". I loved the name, and it was a constant reminder of what Christ did for me. Golgotha is yet another name for Calvary, the place where Christ was crucified, and in Aramaic, it meant "the place of a skull". Can you imagine what Golgotha must have been like? I sure can't. On that fateful day, when Christ was nailed to a tree, it was to Golgotha that he was carrying his cross, and at Golgotha, they gave him wine mixed with gall to drink, but after tasting it, he refused it. It was there they cast lots and divided his clothes and placed a charge above his head: "This is Jesus, the king of the Jews". All of this only makes Golgotha sound like an atrocious, sinful place. But the truth is, Golgotha is where you and I find redemption. It is because of the atrocities at Golgotha that sinners like you and I, can boldly approach the throne of God. Thanks to the sacrifice made by Jesus Christ, we no longer have need to bear our cross; He already bore it for us and has given us eternal access to God the Father. At Golgotha, the weight of our sins stung Christ, but the most anguish he felt, was when he cried, "My God, My God, why hast thou forsaken me?" For the first time in eternity, there was a separation between God the Father and God the Son. Christ clothed himself in our sin, and the Father turned his face away. Christ was separated from his loving Father, because of our sins, and yet he cried out, "Father, forgive them for they know not what they do". There isn't a greater story of love and forgivenesss, than the one at Calvary; if that doesn't grip you, nothing ever will! We sinners find redemption and hope, at Golgotha!

Matthew 27:33-34
And when they came to a place called Golgotha (which means Place of a Skull), they offered him wine to drink, mixed with gall, but when he tasted it, he would not drink it.

Matthew 27:46
And about the ninth hour, Jesus cried out with a loud voice, saying, "*Eli, Eli, lema sabachthani?*" that is, "My God, my God, why have you forsaken me?"

Luke 23:-34
And Jesus said, "Father, forgive them, for they know not what they do."

John 15:13
Greater love has no one than this, that someone lays down his life for his friends.

Philippians 2:6-8
Who, though he was in the form of God, did not count equality with God a thing to be grasped, but emptied himself by taking the form of a servant, being born in the likeness of men. And being found in human form, he humbled himself by becoming obedient to the point of death, even death on a cross.

Romans 5:8-10
But God shows His love for us in that while we were still sinners, Christ died for us. Since, therefore, we have now been justified by His blood, much more shall we be saved by Him from the wrath of God. For if while we were enemies we were reconciled to God by the death of his Son, much more, now that we are reconciled, shall we be saved by His life.

Calvary

O sinner, have you been to Calvary?
Where flows salvation, crimson, free.
For in the Son's cleansing blood,
The Father's grace, descended like a flood.
From the Father, through the Son,
Our peace and victory, forever won.

O sinner, in what is thy boast?
If not in Christ, the Lord of hosts?
Who bore our sin, even wrath, from God,
And yet still stands interceding, as our Lord.
Who, for our sake, humbly gave,
That he might forever, our souls save.

O sinner, why is your soul so weary?
Have you not seen Christ, in all his glory?
Naked, upon the cursed cross, he hung,
With sin's ugly stain, he was stung.
Yet in his anguish, he chose to lovingly cry,
"Father, forgive them; in their stead, I die."

O sinner, why have you lost hope, in what your cling?
If not Calvary, where Christ in agony, did his love to you bring?

A multitude of sins, he covered with forgiveness and love.
For us sinners, forever, he opened heaven's gates above.
O sinner, he gives us hope when there is none at all,
It would do us good, on him only, to call.

Loss

Loss, in every form, is painful, some more so, than others. Losing my niece was devastating; little humans have always been priceless to me, so a little human that was a half of my brother and a half of my sister-in-law was even more precious and thus more devastating. My heart still aches in places joy refuses to reach. What do you do with all that loss, pain, and hurt, but take it to the Lord in prayer? What else do you wonder about when a loved one departs, other than heaven? I am so grateful to God for telling us time and again, in his word, that this is not our end! Death has no victory for those who are in Christ Jesus. While death is the worst thing that can happen to the rest of the world, it is the best thing that can happen to those who believe in Christ. Like Paul said, "For me to live is Christ and to die is gain." But as much as we may have the knowledge of this, when death strikes, you feel the loss, you mourn the loss, the loss will make you ache and pain like never before, but the word of God, will breathe hope into your heart. In this case, my niece will never know of pain, hurt, ache, or sorrow; all she knows is of heaven the place we all long to go; she's already there! So while we mourn the fact that we don't have her here with us, we are confident, she abides in a city that knows no doom or end, and we rejoice in that! There are many days where I wonder what heaven must be like for Ava. I think of Eden and how God said it was all good! Heaven must be far sweeter than Eden. I think of all the gifts all of us would have showered on Ava if she were here, and it still wouldn't come close to the gift of heaven. She gets to reside, where glory dwells! The goodbye was and will forever, be painful, but I know that it is only for a short while. One day Ava and the rest of us in Christ Jesus, will share a home. Amen

Job 3:17-19
There the wicked cease from troubling,
and there the weary are at rest.
There the prisoners are at ease together;
They hear not the voice of the taskmaster.
The small and the great are there,
And the slave is free from his master.

Matthew 19:14
But Jesus said, "Let the little children come to me and do not hinder them, for to such belongs the kingdom of heaven."

2 Samuel 12:23
But now he is dead. Why should I fast? Can I bring him back again? I shall go to him, but he will not return to me."

Revelation 21:4
He will wipe away every tear from their eyes, and death shall be no more, neither shall there be mourning, nor crying, nor pain anymore, for the former things have passed away.

Goodbye Ava

"Goodbye", is not my favourite word,
Especially when it's to a little, tiny you.
Goodbye, just simply makes me ache,
and wish I could everything, better make!
And what if I could have you here?
Just cuddle and tickle and have you near?
Rock you in my arms, to sleep,
Or simply cuddle you and keep?
Ah! Life would be such bliss,
To have you here with me.
And watch you giggle and grow, little miss.
Ava, there's so much I'd love to have done,
I'd have been with you, from dawn, till setting sun.
I'd have loved you with more heart, than I ever have,
And would have enjoyed watching you turn my brother, mad!
Or make your Mom run around, going crazy, and yet certainly
glad!
Ava, you would have filled our family with joy,
You would have been the reason for us, to celebrate every day
and enjoy.
Your parents, grandparents, aunts, uncles, and cousins,
All would have pampered you and brought you gifts by the
dozens.
You would never have wondered about love,
We'd have showered you with it and made you know,

You were a gift from above.
But Ava, we couldn't have what we planned,
Why did God take you, we don't understand!
We know you are with him and always happy and glad,
And yet we cry, because your absence, makes us so sad.
Goodbye for now, my precious, little niece,
Don't ever think I'll forget you, or the missing will ever cease.
I will long for you, until Christ calls me home,
And then in heaven, hand in hand, together we will roam.
I love you, my dear, and always will,
I'll wait to see you, when time stands still!

Making it Count!

We all have numbered days, the Bible teaches us that and life too. We lose people along the way; death is inevitable. Since we know for a fact that death awaits every single one of us, it is important that we make our days count, especially because they are numbered. As Christians, more so. Some of us live our lives in complete oblivion. We think our obedience to Christ is a weekly visit to church, our prayers at home, or giving to the church, missions, poor people, etc. But making our days count is much more than that. It is living a Christlike life. If our testimony at the end of every year is the same, we most likely aren't living entirely as Christ wants us to. If our testimony at the end of the year is about lives changed, about being tested and tried, about loss yet gain in Christ, about learning and leaning on him, then it's safe to say, we are making our numbered days count. We need to be living every day for Christ. If we are living for Christ, we must see fruit. We must see lives being transformed. We must see a change in the ones we are praying for, the ones we are witnessing to, and more importantly, we must see change in ourselves. When Christ is at work in us, we cannot be the same! Remember Paul? He changed drastically, from hating those who followed Christ, to advancing the gospel, for the sake of Christ. That kind of change can only be wrought about by Christ in our life. Lets make our days count, brethren!

Psalm 90:12
So teach us to number our days,
that we may get a heart of wisdom.

John15:4
Abide in me, and I in you. As the branch cannot bear fruit by itself, unless it abides in the vine, neither can you, unless you abide in me.

John 15:8
By this, my Father is glorified, that you bear much fruit and so prove to be my disciples.

John 15:16
You did not choose me, but I chose you and appointed you that you should go and bear fruit and that your fruit should abide, so that whatever you ask the Father in my name, he may give it to you.

Marred Image

She stood before the mirror,
Looking at her face,
Another year gone by,
Wrinkles bore its trace.
But what had she gained, in the year gone by?
Nothing! She realised, with a painful sigh!
Every year, seemed to just, come and go,
Nothing but scars and wrinkles to show.
What was the point, of this meaningless life?
What was the need, of either joy or strife?
Lost in contemplation, she continued to stare,
Hoping she'd find something, worthy of care.
But as she stared, she found, she was only filled with regret,
Of past guilt, and mistakes she could never forget.
The tears began to roll, down her cheek.
Sin, eating into her heart, making her weak.
Staring at her reflection, she was filled with shame.
No accomplishments, absolutely nothing good, to claim.
A sense of hopelessness, but reality, gripped her heart,
Oh! How she wished for a clean slate, a brand-new start!
It was in this moment of weakness, her longing for something
new,
She remembered the words.
"Therefore, if anyone is in Christ, he is a new creation."
The old has passed; behold, the new has come."

She remembered those stories, she had heard several times before,
Except, they were now, more than mere stories; they were now hope, for sure!
She remembered singing: "In weakness, He was all strength,"
She finally opened her Bible and read it at length.
Her pain slowly subsided, with each promise he made,
Her joy, now in Christ, grateful for the redeeming price, he paid.
She looked again into the mirror, to see her face,
This time she saw, only the work of his grace.

Perfect Home

Heaven excites me! It excites me because it is going to be like nothing we've ever seen or had before. None of us have ever enjoyed a place free of sin, but once upon a time, there was such a place and its name was Eden. I heard someone preach on Genesis 1-3 and I was immediately delighted by the thought of Eden. How beautiful it must have been and how happy Adam and Eve must have been, before the sting of sin plagued them!

Eden in all its glory, is but a patch, of the heaven we are assured, in Christ! One day, that beauty, shall be our eternal home.

About Eden:
Genesis 1:31
And God saw everything that he had made, and behold, it was very good.

About Heaven:
Revelation 21:22-27
And I saw no temple in the city, for its temple is the Lord God the Almighty and the Lamb. And the city has no need of sun or moon to shine on it, for the glory of God gives it light, and its lamp is the Lamb. By its light will the nations walk, and the kings of the earth will bring their glory into it, and its gates will never be shut by day—and there will be no night there. They will bring into it the glory and the honour of the nations. But nothing unclean will

ever enter it, nor anyone who does what is detestable or false, but only those who are written in the Lamb's book of life.

Revelation 22: 1-5

Then the angel showed me the river of the water of life, bright as crystal, flowing from the throne of God and of the Lamb through the middle of the street of the city; also, on either side of the river, the tree of life with its twelve kinds of fruit, yielding its fruit each month. The leaves of the tree were for the healing of the nations. No longer will there be anything accursed, but the throne of God and of the Lamb will be in it, and his servants will worship him. They will see his face, and his name will be on their foreheads. And night will be no more. They will need no light of lamp or sun, for the Lord God will be their light, and they will reign forever and ever.

The promise:

Romans 5: 17 -21

For if, because of one man's trespass, death reigned through that one man, much more will those who receive the abundance of grace and the free gift of righteousness reign in life through the one man Jesus Christ. Therefore, as one trespass led to condemnation for all men, so one act of righteousness leads to justification and life for all men. For as by the one man's disobedience the many were made sinners, so by the one man's obedience the many will be made righteous. Now the law came in to increase the trespass, but where sin increased, grace abounded all the more, so that, as sin reigned in death, grace also might reign through righteousness leading to eternal life through Jesus Christ our Lord.

The Garden of Eden

How lovely must that garden have been,
Where God placed Adam and Eve in?
He called it, The Garden of Eden,
The only place that was once free of sin!
That garden, far blessed, than any today,
For God and man fellowshipped every day!
T'was in that garden, that life was born,
Where daylight shone, that very first morn.
It was indeed, very beautiful and bright,
Filled with radiance of our Father's pure light.
Both Man and God, dwelt as one,
Under the glory of, the first sun.
But then one day, sin crept in,
Changed everything from the garden within.
No longer did man, have a home in Eden,
Forsaking God, he had let sin dwell in.
Today we live, in a world, so lost,
We continue to bear, the first man's cost.
God showed Adam, now us, much grace
For He never did erase this human race.
Through one wicked man, sin was brought,
Through the holy Son of Man, sin fought.
No longer do we bear Adam's cost,
In Christ, sin is forever lost.
So as beautiful as Eden may have been,
We look forward to a heaven that knows no sin!

Living for Jesus

Jesus was a man with a mission. He was singularly focused – to buy pardon for mankind and bridge once and for all, the gap between Man and God the Father. Nothing ever came in Jesus' way; actually, He didn't let anything get in his way. Remember Satan tempting him? Satan did try to get in his way, but Jesus had one thing in mind at all times: our salvation. He knew his purpose and He lived up to it while here on earth; now too, in heaven, he is interceding for us. If only we could be like Jesus. We receive salvation and yet so quickly, forget the price at which it came; instead, we are more consumed about the price of the earthly things we think we need, to survive. We get lost in the rat race of life and forget all about the eternity we are called to live and enjoy, from today. Alas, we are not focused like Christ.

Years ago, a friend asked me to write a song for his youth group, and I called it "On Fire for Jesus." It's not just youth who are called to be on fire for Jesus; we are all called to do that! Remember Paul, forsaking all else, he pressed on toward the goal to which he was called, in Christ Jesus! That's how we all ought to be! That's the call for every single one of us who are in Christ Jesus. We are saved to save!

Jude 1:20-23
But you, beloved, building yourselves up in your most holy faith and praying in the Holy Spirit, keep yourselves in the love of

God, waiting for the mercy of our Lord Jesus Christ that leads to eternal life. [22] And have mercy on those who doubt; save others by snatching them out of the fire; to others show mercy with fear, hating even the garment[g] stained by the flesh.

1 Peter 2:9-10

But you are a chosen race, a royal priesthood, a holy nation, a people for his own possession, that you may proclaim the excellencies of him who called you out of darkness into his marvellous light. Once you were not a people, but now you are God's people; once you had not received mercy, but now you have received mercy.

Matthew 28:19-20

Go therefore and make disciples of all nations, baptising them in the name of the Father and of the Son and of the Holy Spirit, teaching them to observe all that I have commanded you. And behold, I am with you always, to the end of the age."

On Fire for Jesus

I heard a story about this man,
Who came to earth to fulfil a plan.
His plan it was, to conquer sin
To die for me and cleanse me within.
Who is this man, do you care to know?
He is Jesus, the ruler evermore.

CHORUS:-
He died for me and buried my sins,
And rose to fulfil my righteous win.
My life to him, I fully owe,
I live on fire for Jesus here below.

This man he did fulfil the plan,
He did this, for every single man.
Both you and I are freed within,
We have conquered both, death and sin.
Accept this Lord, as your own,
He is Jesus, the God who paid your loan.

Now, live your life for this great God,
Live with fire for Jesus our Lord.
He's coming soon to take us home,
No more in sin streets will we roam.
Look we forward, to heaven someday,
But now with fire, we live for Jesus today.

Safe in the Arms of God

A dear friend of mine lost her baby; she had a stillborn in her 8th month. It happened so suddenly that it came as a big shock to all of us. The church rallied around her and her husband. Joy had turned quickly, into sorrow for us all, but we knew there was hope. This happened during the advent season too. Though we all mourned, we knew there was hope. We knew little Ruth had found her way to an eternal home. This happened twenty years ago; today the couple has two lovely kids, both teenagers now. Why God chose to call Ruth home so early, neither they nor any of us know, but this we do know, that God has her safe in his arms. We also know God cares more deeply about his children than we ever could. As special as Ruth was to her parents, she was far more special, to God. He chose her before the foundations of the earth. We also know, God has ordained everyone's time here on earth. God did with Ruth what He had planned, from the beginning. From testimonies of both parents, in hindsight, that trial caused a deeper understanding of God, for both of them, individually. It even strengthened their relationship as a couple. God does use trials to shape us into what he wants us to be. It is when tears fall, that we need comforting, when our sorrow is too large, that we take it to him in prayer, when our heart is torn, that we ask for mending. Trials give us the opportunity to lean on our Father's breast, to be comforted by him.

It is when we are helpless, that we learn, he is true help. Our good God, gives us trials, so we can experience the sweetness of his comfort and peace, which is but the outflow of his Fatherly love, for us. It is in our trials, that we go on bended knee, seeking God but find Father! Trials teach us more, than joy ever could.

Isaiah 43:7
Everyone who is called by my name,
whom I created for my glory,
whom I formed and made.

Psalm 37:8
The Lord knows the days of the blameless,
and their heritage will remain forever.

A Tribute to Ruth

O what joy filled my heart,
When the doctor heard, your little heart.
He told me, it was no longer Daddy and me,
We now were, happy parents to be.
Both Daddy and I, were filled with joy,
We didn't care, if you were a girl or a boy.
Your Dad kept me so happy, my darling,
He listened to my every beckon and calling.
The two of us, were as happy as could be,
Never more in love, than this, were we.
We both always wore happy grins,
Waiting the days, when we'd need diapers and pins.
Then suddenly, it all came to a halt,
Sometimes I wonder, if it were my fault.
Both, Daddy and I, had to run to the doctor,
Something was wrong, death couldn't be the factor!
I was in great pain for most of that night,
But I kept telling myself, when you came out, it would be alright.
Few hours later, the doctor came to me,
I could see the news was not what I wanted it to be.
She told me darling, that you had left me and gone,
My heart ached; I didn't know how, I'd live till the morn.
I still had you inside of me,
I had to bring you out, for the world to see.
When you came out, I held you close to me,
Hoping and silently wishing, I would soon a miracle see.

Daddy and I held you for so long,
You were our precious dream, that came along.
We didn't really get any time with you,
I struggled to accept, that our God best knew.
But in time, God calmed my soul,
He showed me, what was my role.
It wasn't up to me, to decide your timing,
God only chose me, to do all the carrying.
Before Daddy and I, ever thought of you,
God had long chosen, a short life for you.
I wanted to fight with my Maker, my Lord,
But I couldn't, for I knew, you were safe in the arms of God.
Now, time has passed, since then my love,
Our Lord blessed us, with a special gift from above.
Samuel, your little, naughty brother,
Makes us laugh and gives us joy, like no other.
Today, I thank God, for all he has given me,
Not forgetting you, as a precious gift, He gave me.
Your life was short but taught me much,
Because of you, I felt, my Father's tender touch.
Thanks to you, I know, my Father knows best,
This lesson, the depth, of my peace and every rest.

A Woman's Place

Our world today is subject to so much confusion about gender and gender roles. We are falsely told that the Bible advocates inequality between the genders. The Bible doesn't advocate inequality, but it does advocate defined roles for each gender. We were made differently, on purpose, by the one who knows best. That being said, sometimes even well-meaning Christians seem to forget, God created women. He has a purpose for women, much like he does for men. Being a woman does not mean you are called to anything less; you are called to shine for Christ. We have so many examples of wonderful women in the Bible. We have Ruth, we have Phoebe and Priscilla whom Paul makes mention of, and let's not forget when Jesus rose from the dead, he first appeared to the women and entrusted them with the task of telling his disciples that he was alive. Then, one of my favourites – Esther. Esther is a great example to all of us women; she did something that even men would fear; she approached a king, to set God's people free. Remember Moses? He was shy and scared and needed a spokesperson to appear before Pharaoh, but here Esther, a slave made queen, boldly approaches the king, to plead on her people's behalf. You may think Esther had no need to fear since she was the queen approaching her husband? You couldn't be further from the truth! Esther knew that this meeting could cost her, her life; it was against the law, she was not to approach the king. Mordecai had just recently reminded her that while the Jews were doomed, her fate couldn't be much better even though she was in the palace, and he used words that I love, for the next part of his challenge *"And who knows whether you have not come to the kingdom for such a time as this?"*. Esther knew she had to do something, and she did; she found favour in the king's eyes and pleaded for her people, and it was granted. The Jews were rescued because of Esther. Who were the Jews? God's chosen people. God used Esther for his work. Women, we need to let God use us, for his work.

Esther 4: 13-16

"Do not think to yourself that in the king's palace you will escape any more than all the other Jews. For if you keep silent at this time, relief and deliverance will rise for the Jews from another place, but you and your Father's house will perish. And who knows whether you have not come to the kingdom for such a time as this?" Then Esther told them to reply to Mordecai, "Go, gather all the Jews to be found in Susa, and hold a fast on my behalf, and do not eat or drink for three days, night or day. I and my young women will also fast as you do. Then I will go to the king, though it is against the law, and if I perish, I perish."

Esther

Esther was but a pretty young maid,
When the king's men, her city did raid.

All the king's men, many women did take
For Queen Vashti indeed made a mistake.

Vashti's grave mistake cost her, her crown,
And young pretty Esther, was soon brought to town.

The women from Susa, the king's heart were to win,
But pretty young Esther, sent the king's heart for a spin.

Young Esther was given the big, golden crown,
While Queen Vashti's folly, left her with a frown.

Both Vashti and Esther were beautiful indeed,
But Esther, more loved, for her brave deed.

Hearing her people were, to be put to the knife,
Queen Esther went to the throne, no fear for her life.

Riches and honour, she was ready to forsake,
For her great people's, lives were at stake.

She spoiled her dear Lord, with food and wine,
And even asked, wicked Haman, to come dine.

The king and Haman, were both satisfied,
And the Queen's heart, was soon gratified.

The king with great love, half his kingdom did offer,
But Esther only pleaded, for the Jews, not to suffer.

The king, her humble demand did meet,
But his great wrath, against Haman did heat.

Haman was made, to hang on the gallows,
While the Jews' fate, rose from the shallows.

The Jews were saved and their honour restored,
For on Esther, God this great task, had bestowed.

Friend for Sinners

Have you ever been so broken that even tears fail you? It's a rotten feeling. You feel there's not a soul on earth who can share in your pain, because they know nothing of it. You feel justified in your sorrow and pain, because it is unique to you. The Bible tells us a story though, about Jesus. He came down as a man for the very purpose that, we can no longer claim he doesn't know of our pain. Jesus humbled himself and took on the appearance of a man, so he could feel what you and I feel. He makes the perfect friend because he identifies with our sufferings. As terrible as any of our unique sufferings may seem, the truth is, nothing in history is more terrible than Jesus being put to death on a cross! Our suffering, in comparison, is nothing. We know the Bible says that, the wages of sin is death. We know the things that happen, death, illnesses, and other things that plague us, are but the consequences of sin. So in a way, we brought it on ourselves, our sorrow. But Jesus, he was holy, without blemish, yet he chose to become a man, bear our suffering, and give us life anew through salvation, that he gifts us by grace. Who better to go to, with our broken heart, than Jesus? Who can possibly understand us any better than Jesus? He's been in our shoes! He is merciful, kind, compassionate, and forgiving. This is the same Jesus who considered Lazarus his friend and wept at his death and also, was moved to raise him, from the dead. He is the sweetest friend!

Hebrews 2:17-18
Therefore, he had to be made like his brothers in every respect, so that he might become a merciful and faithful high priest in the service of God, to make propitiation for the sins of the people. For because he himself has suffered when tempted, he is able to help those who are being tempted.

Philippians 2:6-8
Who, though he was in the form of God, did not count equality with God a thing to be grasped, but emptied himself by taking the form of a servant, being born in the likeness of men. And being found in human form, he humbled himself by becoming obedient to the point of death, even death on a cross.

Matthew 11:28-30
Come to me, all who labour and are heavy laden, and I will give you rest. Take my yoke upon you, and learn from me, for I am gentle and lowly in heart, and you will find rest for your souls. For my yoke is easy, and my burden is light."

Have You Met Jesus?

Alone in my trials, I stood,
Faking smiles, to keep them misunderstood.
But in my heart, there brewed the deepest pain,
Choking me out of life and any gain.
Solace I found, not even in friend,
This was to be, my bitter, lonely end.
But there he was, that Lamb who was slain,
Calvary's victory, looking down, from holy reign.

Have you met Jesus? Oh, my friend,
He's sweeter than the sweetest friend.
In triumphs, he will, your joy share,
In burdens, he, your refuge and care.
Have you met Jesus? Oh, my friend,
He's sweeter than your sweetest friend.

Dark is the earth, with its cares,
In light, it shall refuse to share.
With worry and sin, it shall plague thee, friend,
Tell you, life is to be lived to the fullest, to the end.
But ne'er shall it tell you, of sin's wretched curse,
That each must pay, with damnation, that is far worse.
The slaughtered Lamb, will let you share in his glory,
O my friend, let him be your only story.

Have you met Jesus? O my friend,
He's sweeter than the sweetest friend.
In triumphs, he will, your joy share,
In burdens, he, your refuge and care.
Have you met Jesus? O my friend,
He's sweeter than your sweetest friend.

With not the faintest sight of hope,
Your trials must seem beyond cope.
For which of us, can change our fate?
Or decide that we can make death, wait?
We have no power, no hold, or say,
Not even to choose our own life's way.
Then what must we find, worth living for?
Except that for which he died?

Have you met Jesus? O my friend,
He's sweeter than the sweetest friend.
In triumphs, he will, your joy share,
In burdens, he, your refuge and care.
Have you met Jesus? O my friend,
He's sweeter than your sweetest friend.

Paraklesis

If you're wondering what paraklesis is, it's the Greek word for 'comfort'. I love that the Bible describes our God as "comfort". How amazing that our God takes time to comfort us in our time of need. I'm not sure how better to explain comfort, than the feeling of an embrace: loving, warm, welcoming arms that wrap you up, in a way that expresses love, possession, and a willingness to shield you from all harm. In today's English, "cwtch" would be the best way to describe it, a Welsh word. That's the kind of comfort we believers get, from the word of God. It is supernatural in the sense that, in the midst of a ridiculously painful trial, with no actual physical arms embracing us, we feel all of that, by just studying the word of God! And so, even on the bleakest of days, when hope seems pointless, when we turn to the word of God, we will find comfort and a peace that passes all understanding. As Christians, sometimes we tend to think, we are most loved by Christ, which makes us feel like he can only want 'good' for us and we do not associate "trials" with "good". The fact that Jesus left us the Comforter, is reason enough for us to know, we will need him. The Christian life is not one, void of trials; it is one filled with trials actually, and that's not saying, God doesn't love us; it's actually because He loves us that he sends trials, to prune us into, who he wants us to be. Here's what we have, the formula, if you will, to beat any trial – to be in Christ Jesus, meaning time in his word! We are not alone. For those who believe in Christ Jesus and have repented from their sins, the Comforter dwells within us. He fills us up with all we need and equips us for every trial. Sometimes, our trial might seem too big, too impossible, but the truth is, nothing is worse than hell, and for those of us in Christ Jesus, we already have victory over hell because of what Christ did at Calvary. If Christ was able to conquer the worst for us, in comparison, what is our current trial? The key to enduring a trial, is knowing, He who is with us is greater, than whatever comes our way. Know, that trials come to shape us into the person God desires us to be. It is trials that help bring about the necessary change in us.

John 14:26

But the Helper, the Holy Spirit, whom the Father will send in my name, he will teach you all things and bring to your remembrance all that I have said to you.

2 Corinthians 1:3-6

Blessed be the God and Father of our Lord Jesus Christ, the Father of mercies and God of all comfort, who comforts us in all our affliction so that we may be able to comfort those who are in any affliction, with the comfort with which we ourselves are comforted by God. For as we share abundantly in Christ's sufferings, so through Christ we share abundantly in comfort too.

Comfort

Broken and hollow,
Without spirit, I fall,
Crushed and crumbling,
My heart cannot handle it all.
This breath, so heavy;
I almost wish it would suddenly cease.
From pain and anxiety,
I only seek, sweet release.
But both, breath or day,
Over them, I cannot have will.
Who am I but clay,
Who the master moulded with skill?

Broken and hollow, that surely cannot be your will?
Crushed and crumbling, that cannot tell of your skill!
Hush, my child, the Spirit speaks to calm,
For your tears and sorrows, there is healing balm.
Who can deliver, but your God, who is all-powerful?
Who can protect, but your Father who fashioned every hour?
Broken, is but art; the Lord creates in you,
Hollow is but heart, the Spirit fills,with comfort anew.
There is nothing under heaven, your great God cannot do,
There is nothing on earth, Satan can do, without God's
permission too.
So take courage, child, your trial is no eternal hell,
Take courage, child, with Jesus, even in trial, it is well!

Emunah

"*Emunah*" is the Hebrew word for "faith." The word implies more than just "trust." The word talks about a faith that is more than mere words; it is a faith that is backed up, with action. We don't talk about faith, we live it, we act it, we do it. *Emunah* is rooted in the knowledge of who God is and is acted out, in true reliance upon God. It doesn't believe that what God says is "true"; it believes "God is truth." Such is the faith, we Christians are called to embrace and demonstrate. Such faith is possible, not because of our understanding or knowledge, but because of the personhood of Christ and his finished sacrifice upon the cross. Chapter 10 of Hebrews explains to us how the law had its constraints and was never really able to cleanse us, once for all, but Christ did what the law could not do: once for all, he offered the sacrifice for all our sins. Because of this, we have confidence; we have a faith that cannot be shaken. And because Christ, once for all, has paid our price, he has also now bridged the gap between Man and God, eternally. No longer is there enmity; we now have the privilege to draw near to God. The closer we draw to God, the more we will desire to know him better. The more we desire to know him, the more he will reveal himself to us, through his word. The more time we spend with his word, the more our hearts and minds will be transformed and cleansed. The more our hearts are transformed, the stronger our faith will become. The stronger our faith, the more immovable it will be. And such faith will not only sanctify us, but will challenge those around us to imitate us. We need Christians in the church to display such faith. It is such faith that spurs one another to love and good works. It is such faith that reminds the brethren that Christ is alive and at work. Christians aren't meant to live a solitary life; we are called to be in the church and be active in the church. We are to cause our brothers and sisters in Christ, to do good works and thus encourage each other. It is at church, where we get to fellowship and live out the joy, of being a family in Christ. It is at church, where we get the opportunity, of corporate worship. We are not to give up on this. The church is the bride of Christ, and He loves her dearly, and we are called to do the same.

Hebrews 10:19-25

Therefore, brothers, since we have confidence to enter the holy places by the blood of Jesus, by the new and living way that he opened for us through the curtain, that is, through his flesh, and since we have a great priest over the house of God, let us draw near with a true heart in full assurance of faith, with our hearts sprinkled clean from an evil conscience and our bodies washed with pure water. Let us hold fast to the confession of our hope without wavering, for he who promised is faithful. And let us consider how to stir up one another to love and good works, not neglecting to meet together, as is the habit of some, but encouraging one another, and all the more as you see the day drawing near.

Steadfast Faith

O Christian, has your faith found resting place,
In Christ's redeeming love and ever abounding grace?
Have you confidence, in the Son's atoning blood,
which at Calvary flowed, a crimson flood?
Have you assurance in it's power to cleanse?
Do you believe, Christ is your defence?

O Christian, is your hope, secure and sound,
Does it know how to stand its ground?
Does it know not to waver, with wind or hail?
Does it know, Jesus is solid rock, not shale.
Oh, know that he who has promised, is faithful,
Oh, know that life without Christ, is fearful.

O Christian, if in Christ, you do believe,
You must his Church, serve and receive.
Love and good works, must flow from you,
Your faith and hope, will prove you true.
And then you'll find, perseverance shall pay,
"He is mine," one day in heaven, Christ shall say!

A Requisition

As Christians, we have but one goal: to be more like Christ. But even that one goal is impossible to achieve, without Christ himself. We go to Christ with the ask, "Make me more like you," and He grants it, because we ask what is pleasing in his sight. All of us who believe in Christ as Saviour. are heaven-bound, but we are called to make our days on earth count. We are called to run the race swiftly for Christ and put him on display, with every stride we take. Satan will do his very best to weaken our stride, slow our race, or make us halt altogether, and he will succeed, if at any point we begin to rest in our own merit and forget, that our power to run, only comes from Christ. Without him, we can do nothing. As followers of Christ, we are to never forget that it is him we lean on, at all times. We run our race daily, by seeking his guidance; we go to him in prayer. Prayer fuels our race and helps us jump, above the hurdles on our path. It is amazing that Christ remains not just the author of our salvation, but the perfecter of our sanctification too. He not only gifts us salvation, but works with us, on our sanctification. Christ has already done immeasurably more than we can ever ask or imagine, and yet, he still allows us to ask of him, and ask we must, to be more like him. Though we have received salvation, sin continues to plague our flesh, and so we continue to do what we don't intend to. Hence, we must take our request before him, ask him to keep us in him and faithful. We must take our cue from history (Bible). Many kings who began their race well, never did complete it or completed it with many halts along the way. From their past, we learn they relied on their strength and didn't look to God. It is not humanly possible for man to remain faithful to God; the law (10 commandments) already taught us that! So how then do we remain faithful? By abiding in Christ Jesus, meaning, relying on him daily, reading his word daily, spending time in prayer daily, memorising scripture, and keeping it hidden in our heart daily! To remain faithful, we need to remain in Christ!

John 15:5

I am the vine; you are the branches. Whoever abides in me and I in him, he is the one that bears much fruit, for apart from me you can do nothing.

Philippians 3:12-14

Not that I have already obtained this or am already perfect, but I press on to make it my own, because Christ Jesus has made me his own. Brothers, I do not consider that I have made it my own. But one thing I do: forgetting what lies behind and straining forward to what lies ahead, I press on toward the goal for the prize of the upward call of God in Christ Jesus.

Proverbs 16:3

Commit your work to the Lord,
And your plans will be established.

1 Samuel 15:26

And Samuel said to Saul, "I will not return with you, for you have rejected the word of the Lord, and the Lord has rejected you from being king over Israel."

Adjuration

Filthy and vile, Lord, I come to thee,
Cleanse my heart, set me free.
Strip away all that makes me, me,
Clothe me with what can make me like thee.

Wretched and sinful, I can no longer be,
For in thy grace, I now salvation receive.
Sin and self, nailed to that wretched tree,
Righteousness, my inheritance, that thou didst give me.

And in thy strength, Lord, strive I shall,
To run my race faithfully, even when life is dull.
And one fine day, sin no more, my fight shall be,
For I shall dwell where your glory engulfs me.

And until that day, dear Lord, keep me, I pray,
Prone to wander, let me from your fold, never stray!
Keep my feet, resting, on Christ, my solid ground,
Keep me running swiftly, always, only, heaven-bound.

Come Undone

What a privilege, as Christians, we enjoy! We have that unique right to go before the Father, Son and Spirit and lay whatever is on our mind. We get to plead, cry, beg and reveal whatever is on our heart. Even human relationships don't allow us that privilege. With man, we always fear our honesty would hurt or cause irreparable damage, but not so with God. We go to God in all honesty; we get to exercise complete transparency, even express our disbelief about him, to him, and we can do all of this without fear, because not only is he our God, but he is also our loving Father. God first loved us; we didn't earn his love. He loves us even when we reveal our weak hearts but express a desire to be his. God cares about our sanctity, more than even we do. God welcomes us to bring what's on our heart to him, however trivial or profound it may be. He listens. Our every sin, our broken dreams, our every pain, our magnificent trial, our annoying doubt, our weary soul – we can take it all to God in prayer. I have had times of disbelief and wondering of how to make sense of God's sovereignty, in the midst of difficult times, and the lyrics of that beautiful hymn by Fanny Crosby, "*Pass me not O gentle Saviour*," come to mind. I love the verse that says "*Let me at Thy throne of mercy find a sweet relief, kneeling there in deep contrition, Help my unbelief.*" I love how Fanny reminds us that even the "power to believe" is not of us; it is from God. That is why we take even our disbelief, to him in prayer. Faith is a gift from God; it is not of us. Ephesians 2 emphasises that. "*What a friend we have in Jesus*" is yet another hymn that reminds us of the privilege we have to take everything to God in prayer. Joseph Scriven penned it so beautifully, "*O what peace we often forfeit, O what needless pain we bear, all because we do not carry everything to God in prayer.*" Christians, let us exercise this God-given right and take everything to our dear Lord in prayer – the good, the bad, and the ugly.

John 16:24

Until now, you have asked nothing in my name. Ask, and you will receive, so that your joy may be full.

Philippians 4:6-7

Do not be anxious about anything, but in everything by prayer and supplication with thanksgiving, let your requests be made known to God. And the peace of God, which surpasses all understanding, will guard your hearts and your minds in Christ Jesus.

1 John 5:14-15

And this is the confidence that we have toward him, that if we ask anything according to his will, he hears us. 15 And if we know that he hears us in whatever we ask, we know that we have the requests that we have asked of him.

Ezekiel 36: 25-27

I will sprinkle clean water on you, and you shall be clean from all your uncleannesses, and from all your idols I will cleanse you. And I will give you a new heart, and a new spirit I will put within you. And I will remove the heart of stone from your flesh and give you a heart of flesh. And I will put my Spirit within you, and cause you to walk in my statutes and be careful to obey my rules.

My Cry

Would you hear me, Lord, if I cried tonight?
Would you calm my heart and pour some light?
Would you give me peace that passes understanding?
Would you show me again, solid is the rock, on which I'm standing?
Would you speak to me, as a friend of old?
Would you show me, your word is richer, than even pure gold?
Would you touch my soul and heal my sinful fear?
Would you fulfil your promise and keep me, ever near?
Would you ignite again, that fire that once burned in me?
Would you change me, so that the world, more of you, in me can see?
Would you love me, Lord, as only you can love?
Would you teach me, Lord? You give good things from above!
Would you show me, Lord, that time is reference, only for man?
Would you prove to me, that eternal, is your plan!
Would you grow faith, even in my sinking heart?
Would you make alive that promise, "Nothing shall ever tear us apart!"
Would you show to me, Lord, that you are not just friend and God,
Would you show me again, you are kind Father, who knows my step, my trod!
Would you guide me, Lord, to higher ground?
Would you give me eyes, for heaven and nothing else around?

Would you strengthen me, Lord, when the race gets rough?
Would you show me again, with you, nothing is tough!
Would you bind me, God, yours forever to be?
Would you keep me in Christ, to live, forever free?

In His Image

"In his image," that phrase is profoundly extravagant. That God the Father, the omnipotent, omniscient, omnipresent God, would make us "in his image" is flabbergasting, mind-boggling, and also extremely humbling. We bear the image of God; that alone should steer us, into appreciating every minute detail, about ourselves. But alas, we live in a world that defines beauty as something altogether different, than what God intended it to be. We live in a world that wants to standardise beauty; it tells us what is the perfect length of a nose, how wide a smile ought to be, how tiny our waist should be, and so on. "Different" is not appreciated. Weighed down by these ridiculous standards of beauty, so many people forget they are more than, what meets the eye. We are created "In his image," both men and women alike. The Bible says, we are fearfully and wonderfully made. Our mighty God, the creator of all things, the things that we see – like the magnificent mountains, glorious skies, the gorgeous sunsets – knitted us together, in our mother's womb painstakingly; he made us just like we ought to be. He has made us each, different and unique, on purpose, according to his will. How can we then, not be content with who we are? In 1 Samuel, we are reminded that unlike us, God looks at the "heart" for beauty. He doesn't look at the outward appearance. Throughout the Bible, we see that the heart is what defines who a man or woman is. Instead of spending our time perfecting or improving our outward appearance, we ought to be grooming our heart, making it a place worthy of God's dwelling. As Christians, we believe the spirit of God resides in us, within our heart; then should we not be adorning our heart with beauty?

Genesis 1:27
So God created man in his own image, in the image of God he created him; male and female he created them.

1 Samuel 16:7
But the Lord said to Samuel, "Do not look on his appearance or on the height of his stature, because I have rejected him. For the Lord sees not as man sees: man looks on the outward appearance, but the Lord looks on the heart."

Matthew 6:14
For if you forgive others their trespasses, your heavenly Father will also forgive you.

Psalm 51:10
Create in me a clean heart, O God, and renew a right spirit within me.

Matthew 5:7-8
Blessed are the merciful, for they shall receive mercy. "Blessed are the pure in heart, for they shall see God."

Cut by the Knife

He who knows, has carved well,
He foresees, he sees swell.
He frames his sculpture,
No piece he fractures.
His beauty not noticed, for ill want from life,
People simply crave beauty, cut by the knife.

He who knows, makes the heart,
Makes everyone, uniquely apart,
He concentrates not, on colour and skin,
He cares more, about heart and sin.
Yet some tend to think, they need more from life,
They simply need outward beauty, cut by the knife.

He who is the creator is gifted with skill,
For who else could make something, from nil.
He does not judge, based on our face,
For his beauty exists, in the extent of his grace.
People are blind; they don't look beyond this life,
They need temporary beauty, cut by the knife.
And people who live, to be cut by the knife,
Never find beauty, nor love in this life.
If beauty is only, in what is begotten,
It will soon fade away, it will be forgotten.
Forgiveness, love, grace, and mercy, true beauty in life,
All, freely given in Christ. No need to be, cut by the knife!

Home Away from Home

I was about 18 when the idea of going to a land where no one knew me, plagued me. I wanted to do that because I wanted to put my faith to the test. Growing up in a Christian home, I knew all the right answers to the most common questions Christians pose to unbelievers, to check, if they believe. I feared my answers might simply be "answers". I really did want, to test my faith, on this side of heaven and know, with certainty, that when I said "Lord, Lord," He would hear me. Here at home, I was surrounded by so many people and despite being fiercely independent, if I needed anything, I had only to ask the zillion that surrounded me. After hearing so often from Corinthians to "examine myself" and test if I'm in the faith, I felt like I needed to do it. "All that thrills my soul is Jesus" and "It is well" were hymns I loved, and I wanted to test if I really meant those two hymns and if I'd still sing them with gusto, in the midst of trials. I prayed for this and at 23, God answered. I packed my bags and went to Hungary, and what a way God answered my prayer! For the record 12 months I was there, I had a trial for every month, some tiny, some humungous! One of them - I am diabetic and have been for 21 years; I live on 4 insulin injections a day. Back in Hungary, I ran out of insulin, and my type of insulin was no longer being produced there. Since I was 17, I had not gone a single meal without insulin, so the crisis, was very real, threatening to be fatal. Besides that, to get insulin, I needed insurance, a local doctor, or a prescription; I had none of that either, but God provided! God taught me to call on him in times of need; my folks back home didn't always know the mess I was in! I learnt to trust Jesus and indeed found him sweet. Despite all the different trials I encountered, Hungary soon became home; I learnt to joy in this foreign land, because I found Jesus nearer and sweeter than ever before. And after all these years, Hungary is still a place that is home.

This is the poem I wrote in the first month of me moving there when I was still so terribly homesick. I wanted to come home and never travel away from home, ever again. But in that foreign land, God provided a fantastic church, great friends, and opportunities to minister. My testimony after 12 months in Hungary was, that I would now miss this new home, back in my own country. The fellowship of believers is a blessed thing; strangers become family and while cultural differences exist, unity beyond understanding, is sealed in the brotherhood of Christ.

Genesis 1:21
Now the Lord said to Abram, "Go from your country and your kindred and your Father's house to the land that I will show you."

Psalm 119:147
I rise before dawn and cry for help;
I hope in your words.

2 Corinthians 12:9
But he said to me, "My grace is sufficient for you, for my power is made perfect in weakness." Therefore, I will boast all the more gladly of my weaknesses, so that the power of Christ may rest upon me.

Joy in A Foreign Land

Here in a foreign land,
All alone, cold, I stand.
Afraid of what lies ahead,
Weary, I lay down my head.

I seek familiar, friendly faces,
But all I find are different races.
Driven to tears, I am prone to bawl,
But instead, humbly at His feet I fall.

My God, My God,
You are Lord,
Whether in a foreign land or at home,
Never from your presence can I roam.

You have been my guide in life,
Sent me both, joy and strife,
In you alone, I find hope and stay,
Be my joy forever and this day.

And in your joy, this land I'll love,
Look at each moment, as a gift from above.
Your peace will flood my heart and mind,
I'll learn to treasure you, and leave people behind.

So thank you, Lord, for this distant land,
Thank you for your comforting hand.
I need no familiar face,
For I rest on your all-sufficient grace.

Answered Prayer

There is great joy in answered prayer, isn't it? Getting what we want, that's what we reckon is answered prayer, but we couldn't be further from the truth. Sometimes, prayers are answered in ways we could have never imagined. It is nothing like we wanted and yet it is what we asked for. Let me explain. My brother and his wife, like the rest of the family, prayed that they would have a baby. My brother and his wife had more specific prayers for their baby. They prayed that God would bless them with a daughter, they prayed she would be as beautiful as her mother, that she would have "rosebud" lips like her Father and above all else, that she would be a child who knows God in the true sense, that she would have the gift of salvation and share eternity with Christ. Now, that's an amazing prayer to have as a parent, isn't it, especially for an unborn child? Neither the parents, nor us the family, realised, the granting of this request would come, in the form of Ava being stillborn. Never did we imagine, that our prayers would be answered, by Ava enjoying Christ before us, or us having to bear, the unbelievable agony of not getting to watch her grow, crawl, walk, run, cry, giggle, laugh, talk and more! Suddenly, we were granted everything we asked for and yet nothing we envisioned. We envisioned a long, dear life for Ava. She, being our baby girl filled with joy. We imagined we'd spoil her rotten with love, dress her up in the prettiest of clothes, cuddle and hug her tight, every single day of her life, go on holidays with her, enjoy her grow from baby to toddler to teen, young lady and then woman, and in God's time, be blessed watching her embrace Christ. But that's not what we got!

Ava was more beautiful than my feeble words can ever describe. In the truest sense, an angel we met and now she abides with Christ, in his heavenly home. We know Ava is happy where she is; we don't doubt that for one minute. Are we happy? Yes and No! Happy, that prayers were unanswered, broken, because we miss her. But the same God who answered our prayer for Ava, we know that he is at work, within all our grieving hearts and is working out, what is pleasing to him, even through this loss. Heaven has always been dear because of its promise of Christ and sinlessness; now a reunion with Ava, is also what thrills me! Like Hannah, our prayers were answered, just differently!

John 16:24
Until now, you have asked nothing in my name. Ask, and you will receive, so that your joy may be full.

1 John 5: 14-15
And this is the confidence that we have toward him, that if we ask anything according to his will, he hears us. And if we know that he hears us in whatever we ask, we know that we have the requests that we have asked of him.

1 Samuel 1:27-28
For this child, I prayed, and the Lord has granted me my petition that I made to him. Therefore, I have lent him to the Lord. As long as he lives, he is lent to the Lord."

For this Child I Prayed

There's a prayer that came to pass,
When the doctor said to us at last,
Congratulations, you both are parents to be,
Our eyes lit up; the delight, the whole world could see!

There's a prayer that came to pass,
A baby would soon be ours.
Ours to hold, to cuddle, and enjoy,
To be our hope, love, and forever joy.

There's a prayer that came to pass,
That our baby would be a little lass,
That she'd be as pretty as her mother,
That she'd have lips, just like her Father.

There's a prayer that came to pass,
Ava, our little precious lass,
Everything her mother had hoped her to be.
Everything her Father had dreamed she'd be.

There's a prayer that came to pass,
That Ava would know God as first and last,
So before she, our faces could see,
She was taken to heaven, in glory to be.

There's a prayer that came to pass,
Ava, now God's eternal lass.
No pain, no tears, no grief she'll ever know,
Her face shall only hold God's eternal glow.

There's a prayer that shall soon come to pass.
Where we shall find, our Saviour and our lass,
In glory, we shall all joyfully forever be.
Never wanting, never wailing, just complete and free.

Cobbled Streets

I love walking. I can spend hours in the day, walking around, admiring nature. In fact, it's my favourite thing to do when I travel. I find it's the best way to get the local experience and explore the city. I realised I loved walking only when I moved to Eger. Initially, walking around Eger was a necessity since I lived near the city square where transportation wasn't allowed, and I needed to be wise about how I spent my money. But in time, I realised I enjoyed walking; it cleared my head. A few feet from my house were cobbled streets, that led to a palace nearby. I enjoyed walking down that street in particular. Reading revelations often made me think of heaven and try to picture what heaven would be like. While the gems seemed fascinating, I kept thinking meeting my heroes from the Bible would be the most thrilling thing in heaven. It would be bringing my bedtime stories as a kid, back to life. Heaven thrills me for the promise of Christ and his glory, but also for all these men and women whom I have grown to love and admire. I can't imagine sharing the same heaven as all these people! Heaven is going to be so fascinating; it's going to be an eternity of someone granting me my every wish! How incredibly wonderful is that?! The more I think about heaven, the more exciting it gets, and death seems far from scary. Instead, I long to hear like the dying thief, "today, you shall be with me in paradise".

Revelations 21:14
And the wall of the city had twelve foundations, and on them were the twelve names of the twelve apostles of the Lamb.

Revelations 21:21
And the twelve gates were twelve pearls, each of the gates made of a single pearl, and the street of the city was pure gold, like transparent glass.

Luke 23:43
And he said to him, "Truly, I say to you, today you will be with me in paradise."

1 Thessalonians 4:16-17
For the Lord himself will descend from heaven with a cry of command, with the voice of an archangel, and with the sound of the trumpet of God. And the dead in Christ will rise first. Then we who are alive, who are left, will be caught up together with them in the clouds to meet the Lord in the air, and so we will always be with the Lord.

Joyous Heaven

Into the gates of heaven, I shall walk, One fine day,
Greeting those saints of old, who encouraged me on my way!
And as I enter, I shall stop to greet and meet,
The lives that spurred me, on earth's narrow, winding street.
There I shall, that great patriarch see,
O Abraham! Thy faith, to righteousness but a key.
That thou wouldst leave land and all,
Simply to obey, Yahweh's holy call?!
I shall marvel at this blessed one,
From whom was born every Christian son.
I shall glory in his faith and, to him tell,
How beautiful, that he wouldst offer even only son,
Believing Yahweh could make all things, new and well.

And onward I shall go, smiling at every other saint,
Rejoicing in heaven's beauty,
Far richer than images my feeble mind could ever paint.
And as I onward go, I shall finally stop by Joseph,
To thank him for his rich words
"That Man should mean for us harm, But God, everything for
our good".
His honesty and forgiveness, O What a lesson for me,
For in his life, imitation of the Holy One I did see.

I shall continue on my way, until Moses I have found,
I shall sit by his side, eager to hear his shy words, Ah! The sweet sound.
O Moses! Thou art my hero, from beginning to the end,
For thou didst commune with God, as friend with friend.
Dear Moses, on thy words, so often I have meditated,
"Show me your glory!" How often my sinful heart has penetrated.
That thou didst desire God so much, my soul it ever awakened,
That thy God is simply my God, my soul it ever renewed.
O Moses! Pharaoh's wealth, thou didst willingly give up,
But Ah! The sea of treasures thou dost now have,
Overflowing, thy blessed, eternal cup.
I shall sit there with him awhile, glorying in the stories of old,
For his faith, far richer to me, than even the purest of gold.

And on my way as I go, I shall stop when I hear the harp,
For my soul shall rejoice when I hear, David play a minor or a sharp.
Ah! To finally see "The One After God's own heart"
To hear from him and understand, what truly set him apart!
David, O thou brave soul! To conquer Goliath, with but sling and stone,
Thou didst what king and army feared, thou didst conquer for Yahweh's glory alone.
Thy story, O David, so real, rich and true,
From rags to riches, sin to glory, in his kindness, you forever grew.
And of all kings, thou wouldst be simply great,
For Jesus be born of thine lineage, such was thy granted fate.

And there, both David and I shall rejoice and sing,
With song and heart, we shalt worship our God and King.

And when I see David smile with pride,
I'll know, Solomon has joined beside.
O Solomon, thy words, so rich and pure,
T'was life to the dead, to the sick, simply cure.
That thou didst ask for wisdom, to me such a marvel,
That thou didst ask for wisdom, a truth I still grapple.
I love thee for building, our Father's temple, his home,
I love thee for teaching, that wealth will but, from man to man, roam.
Thou didst say "Fear God, there shall all thy wisdom begin",
Thou didst say "Fear God and obey, from thine very youth begin".

Content with the beauty, that in heaven surrounds.
I'll walk the jewelled streets, gazing happily around.
When I hear friendship's sweet chime, I shall make yet another halt,
For Shadrach, Meshach, Abednego, and Daniel,
Great heroes of their time, to the earth, perfect salt.
O! such mighty faith, to be thrown into the lion's den,
O! such mighty faith, to be thrown into a fiery furnace.
O! such lovely friendship, to pray in unity,
O! such lovely friendship, to obey Yahweh without ambiguity.
I shall to them tell, thy faith, Ah! Simply magnificent,
I shall to them tell, thou didst make death, completely insignificant.

And onward I shall continue, on those precious streets,
Beside humble saints, occupying empty seats.
Listening to their glorious tales,
Of how Yahweh led them but never did fail.
I shall with them glory in our God,

Praise him, for being our sovereign Lord.
And all the saints shall bless his name,
I'll do the same and look for him, who taught me to do the same.
O Job! Thy story, my heart has always blest,
In trials, thine assurance in God, taught me sweet rest.
"The Lord giveth and the Lord taketh away", from thee I did learn,
Thy life, contentment in my heart did churn.

Then I'll continue on my way, with a blest heart,
Until I meet that saint who hath revealed to me, that God hath
set me apart.
O Peter! How I love thee for being just like me,
O Peter! How I love thee, for in thee, Christ I did see.
O That thou didst hear Christ's voice and simply followed,
O That thou didst hear his words and his message, simply
echoed.
O That thou didst sin and fall terribly short of his glory,
O That thou didst repent, follow, and even in death live his story.
O Peter! Thou hast so often, blest my weary heart,
O Peter, we his blessed priesthood, by grace, set apart.

With joyful heart I shall continue, to take even stride,
Enjoying the blessed company, of the saints who walk beside.
And when finally, I meet Paul, who once was known as Saul,
My heart shall grow weak with emotion, but with pride It'll stand
up tall.
O Saul! That Christ doth save and change, I learnt from thy call,
For Christ alone could change, a heartless Saul, to a Paul.
From thee I learnt, Christ maketh all things new.
From thee I learnt, Christ loveth both Gentile and Jew.
And I'll say to Paul, with most humble heart,

"Thank you, thank you for it all"
Thy words of wisdom and rich imagery,
Oft revealed, the crucified Christ of Calvary.
In thy letters, my God I always found,
In thy letters, the joy of how, I'm heaven bound.
Thy letters, revealed my wicked sin,
Thy words breathed life,
By grace, I'm saved through Christ's eternal win.
So thank you, O precious one, for the life thou once didst live,
For thy story, in mine trails, great confidence didst give.

And as I continue with determined stride, upon heaven's perfect
streets,
I shall long to see him who in visions, often Christ did meet.
And when I find John, O that beloved one,
To be one of the disciples, and also to have Christ's love won.
Thou didst teach me, much about Christ's love,
Thou didst teach me, to love, is to be like mine God above.
Obedience, yet another lesson from thee I did learn,
From thine letters, great wisdom I did earn.

And just as I think, I've seen most of heaven's beauty,
I'll hear the saints and angels sing
"Holy, Holy, Holy, O Lamb of God, only thou art worthy!".
It is then that I shall know that heaven, is better than any story,
It is then that I shall truly understand, all there is to glory.
For there before me, shall lie light, like no other,
For there before me shall be the One, who is like no other.
And with joyful heart, I shall prostrate fall, upon that holy ground,
Singing loud Hallelujahs, with all the heavenly hosts around.

And all that I hath seen in heaven, shall simply mean nothing,
For on his throne, I shall see, my God, my Maker, my King, my Everything.
And years shall flash before mine eyes, but ne'er shall I tire,
From worshipping him who lies upon heaven's perfect seat.
There in heaven, I shall fulfil all of my life's destiny,
For I shall worship and praise the Lamb upon the throne, from then until eternity.

Go Tell

C.H. Spurgeon is one of my all-time favourite authors. Not only do I love his content, but I also love his style of writing. "The Soul-Winner" is such a great read. The need of the hour is evangelism. In my few decades here on earth, I've been privy to the Kargil war, tsunami, 9/11 attack, 26/11 Mumbai attack, Taliban's rule, tumult in Syria, Covid, several earthquakes, Ukraine & Russia war, Israel & Hamas war, instability in Iraq, terrorism in Kashmir, and so much more. Every single event caused the loss of lives, lives that may not have known the Bible revealed God. The world needs Christ, and we have been commanded to give all men Christ! The world is growing old in sin and hatred, and we Christians are failing them! We are failing our God-given task of spreading the gospel. We were saved to snatch sinners from hell. All of us, our days are numbered, meaning, there is an appointed time for our death. We won't get a minute less or a minute more. Every day we live, brings us that much closer, to our end. Our time will soon be up, so let's make our time here count! Let's tell everyone we know about Jesus, the Saviour they need. Let's be like Andrew in John Chapter 1, who barely comes to know Jesus is the Messiah and is off telling his brother, Simon Peter, and brings him to Jesus too. Like Spurgeon reminds us, you don't need doctrine to save people; you just need to give them Christ.

Isaiah 52:7
Preach the word; be ready in season and out of season; reprove, rebuke, and exhort, with complete patience and teaching.

Matthew 5:16
In the same way, let your light shine before others, so that[b] they may see your good works and give glory to your Father who is in heaven.

Matthew 9:37-38
Then he said to his disciples, "The harvest is plentiful, but the labourers are few; therefore, pray earnestly to the Lord of the harvest to send out labourers into his harvest."

Romans 10:13
For "everyone who calls on the name of the Lord will be saved."

1 Timothy 2:3-6
This is good, and it is pleasing in the sight of God our Saviour, who desires all people to be saved and to come to the knowledge of the truth. For there is one God, and there is one mediator between God and men, the man[a] Christ Jesus, who gave himself as a ransom for all, which is the testimony given at the proper time

2 Timothy 4:2
Preach the word; be ready in season and out of season; reprove, rebuke, and exhort, with complete patience and teaching.

Evangelism

The world is running out of time, Lord,
And I'm here, simply sinning.
The world is running out of time, Lord,
And I'm stupidly grace spending.
The world is running out of time, Lord,
And the devil's simply winning.
The world is running out of time, Lord,
And men are dying.
The world is running out of time, Lord,
Their souls are ever fading,
The world is running out of time, Lord,
Their end is soon beginning.
The world is running out of time, Lord,
Oh! Help me, I'm begging.
To rid myself of sin, self, and fear,
To never forget, that doom is sure and near,
To snatch my brothers from the fire,
To work for you, them, and never tire.
To love the lost, as if, they were my own,
To lead them to your forgiving throne.
To show them, there is always light,
To help them, drop their scales and gain sight.
To lead them to, bloody Calvary,

To let them know, they can gain righteousness, justly.
The world is running out of time, Lord,
And I'm selfishly living.
The world is running out of time, Lord,
Help me be watchful and ever-giving.

A Pandemic

Covid-19 was like nothing I had ever seen or heard about before. I remember wondering what the big fuss was about, when my organisation declared mandatory work from home that week in March '20. I was keen to go to the office to finish some pending work but was told I wouldn't be allowed in. I thought, "Oh well! I can't fight the system; I'll get to completing the work next week." Not in my wildest dreams did I think, the pandemic would span over so many years. I hear people are still dying from Covid or the vaccine's after effects.

The next poem was written a few months into Covid-19 and quarantine. I remember how terrified so many people were. So many refused to even step out of their house, for the fear of Covid. I remember reading news reports of cadavers unclaimed because people were terrified, to even bury their loved ones who died from Covid. Seeing how scared the world was and their lack of faith in a God who could do immeasurably more than they could ask or imagine, led me to write the poem. I wanted so badly for the world to find, even in the midst of this pandemic, that felt like "sinking sand", that there was solid ground to be found, in Christ. That great hymn of old kept chiming in my head: "*On Christ the solid rock I stand, all other ground is sinking sand, all other ground is sinking sand.*" I wanted the world to know and have calm and peace, in the midst of this pandemic that was simply chaotic. I can't say I wasn't scared of Covid, but my fear was not in the fact that death could strike us; it was in the fact that death could strike people I love who may not yet know Christ and his redeeming love.

John 14:27
Peace I leave with you; my peace I give to you. Not as the world gives do I give to you. Let not your hearts be troubled, neither let them be afraid. You heard me say to you, 'I am going away, and I will come to you.'

Matthew 7:24-25
"Everyone then who hears these words of mine and does them will be like a wise man who built his house on the rock. And the rain fell, and the floods came, and the winds blew and beat on that house, but it did not fall, because it had been founded on the rock."

Luke 6:47-48
Everyone who comes to me and hears my words and does them, I will show you what he is like: he is like a man building a house, who dug deep and laid the foundation on the rock. And when a flood arose, the stream broke against that house and could not shake it, because it had been well built.

Covid19

In the wake of a morning dull,
My helpless world thinks God's power is null!
Death, it has plagued their homes and hearts.
Terrified the masses and torn them apart.
Troubled waters, lie all around,
Teach them, Lord,
You are rock, solid ground!

With bitter dreams, they sleep at night,
Not knowing, where to find, true light.
The sun comes up, but they fear its ray,
This virus can make any man its prey.
Quicksand is all around,
Teach them, Lord,
You are rock, solid ground!

In their own homes, they helpless stay,
Wondering, if death will make its way.
The rich, they find, no hope in wealth,
The poor, they worry, theirs is ill health.
The end of man seems to lurk around,
Teach them, Lord,
You are rock, solid ground!

Purposeful Life

Some of us think of our "being saved" as the end of our story, but hey Christian, it is only our beginning! The days before, are not even worthy of count, but we are saved, so we can make the days after, count! That's not saying we earn our way to heaven. But sinners are saved to save! We are called to evangelise. We are called to bear fruit. We are called to be the light; the world doesn't know of yet. Remember Jesus, he charged his disciples with taking the gospel to the ends of the earth and they did! We are given the same charge, all of us who believe in Christ. We are called to take his word to the ends of the earth. Time is running out, the world is growing old in sin, we are called to be the light they need. We need to stop looking at our salvation, as a confirmed seat in heaven, but instead, honour that grace that saved us, by telling of it, to whomever we meet. We need to let the world know we are Christian. We need to live it out with heart, action, word and let our brothers and sisters experience the same grace. Yes, our world is stubborn and sinful but don't forget, we were exactly that. Remember Sodom? Remember Abraham's prayer? Every time God spoke of destruction, Abraham tried a new bargain, what's more, God listened! Pray and plead with God for the salvation of our family and friends. Be to them, what Abraham was to Lot. Abraham began pleading for Sodom, asking God to spare them if there were at least 50 righteous people, he kept pleading and even asked for pardon if there were only 10 righteous people and God agreed. We need to go before God with confidence, he grants prayers that are according to his will. God showed Lot kindness for the sake of Abraham.

Genesis 19:29
So it was that, when God destroyed the cities of the valley, God remembered Abraham and sent Lot out of the midst of the overthrow when he overthrew the cities in which Lot had lived.

1 John 5:14-15
And this is the confidence that we have toward him, that if we ask anything according to his will, he hears us. And if we know that he hears us in whatever we ask, we know that we have the requests that we have asked of him.

Matthew 28:19-20
Go therefore and make disciples of all nations, baptising them in[b] the name of the Father and of the Son and of the holy Spirit, teaching them to observe all that I have commanded you. And behold, I am with you always, to the end of the age."

John3:16-19
"For God so loved the world, that he gave his only Son, that whoever believes in him should not perish but have eternal life. For God did not send his Son into the world to condemn the world, but in order that the world might be saved through him. Whoever believes in him is not condemned, but whoever does not believe is condemned already, because he has not believed in the name of the only Son of God. And this is the judgement: the light has come into the world, and people loved the darkness rather than the light because their works were evil."

Purpose

Christ died on a cursed cross.
To spread salvation across.
And through his atoning blood,
Righteousness came in like a flood.
He chose us, his followers, to be,
Have you ever wondered, "Why me?"

And while you ponder on the, why me?
Turn to his word, and you will clearly see.
You are saved to save,
You are called, Christlike to behave.

Your soul, on the cruel cross, was won,
You are to win, every single lost son.
You are called, to snatch from the fire,
Not to lose any brother or sister, to the pier!

So stop wasting time and witness to all,
See your brethren, before your king, fall.
Live your life, saints to make,
Do not let them fall into the fiery lake!

Your call is to evangelise,
Stop living, just to socialise!

Wake up! So many are perishing,
Stand guard, and win the dying.

Your purpose here is, souls to win,
You are at war against, ever-increasing sin.
So press on, Christian, with undying love,
Win ye souls, for your Father up above!

Suffering Saint

The Bible tells us that suffering gives us the privilege of identifying with Christ. Being tested through trial, belongs to those who are in Christ, for through the trial and our endurance, we can bring him glory. There are plenty of people mentioned in the Bible who went through great trials, but when you think of trial and endurance, Job is the name that stands up tall. It is difficult to express at the death of a loved one - "He giveth and He taketh away, blessed be the name of the Lord" and yet that was Job's response after losing all his children. I am not even considering the wealth he lost, because as poor as I am, I'd rather lose the little I have and still have the ones I love, than the other way around. So I am sure, the grief of losing his children, overpowered his grief, of losing his wealth. Yet, through all of this, Job was able to see God was sovereign and still bless his name. Job was righteous. It is also interesting to learn from Job's life that Satan didn't just have the power to do what he pleased with Job; he needed God's permission. That's another lesson for us all: trials come with God's knowledge and permission. It isn't something that just happens by accident. Satan was crafty as always and makes mention that everyone regards their own life as precious, so God allowed him to cause Job's body to be covered in sores. This time, Job's trial was not around him, it was on him, within him, and we see that slowly, his confidence in the Lord fades. The friends around him lacked wisdom in their advice. They didn't help turn Job's eyes to the

Lord. In the midst of this new trial, we see Job loses hope, until a friend, Elihu, points him back to the Lord. Another lesson for us: embrace those who make you fix your eyes on Christ. Job's account is joyful for so many reasons, one in particular – honesty. Job, though righteous, has a momentary lapse; in the midst of his trial, he needs reminding and receives it from a friend, who points out to him that God is sovereign. Trials refine our faith like nothing else ever can. It takes enduring trial, to have a faith, that's worthy of glorifying Christ. Gold catches our eye, even from a distance, especially pure gold. The purest form of gold is obtained only when refined through scorching fire. Trials are the fire God uses to refine our faith and make it into a substance that attracts believers and unbelievers alike! Our faith through trial, tells more of Christ than our unending, loud Amens during times of joy or our many rattling of verses, as testimony or our loud singing, of doctrinally sound hymns. Trials cause growth and wisdom in our heart; it is the inward work, that God uses to cause outward beauty. It testifies of the existence of God. After my niece's funeral, I heard many friends say, your family's faith spoke volumes to us. Job endured; that was his testimony and in doing so, he glorified God. We don't run from trial but treasure it because we know God is using it to build our faith, God is using it for his glory.

1 Peter 4:12-13

Beloved, do not be surprised at the fiery trial when it comes upon you to test you, as though something strange were happening to you. But rejoice insofar as you share Christ's sufferings, that you may also rejoice and be glad when his glory is revealed.

Job

Trials, they come, many our way,
Some to pass and some to stay.
But every trial, a lesson will bring,
You must choose, to Christ or sin, to cling?
Trials, they come, to make you strong,
Remember Job? His trial was long.
But why, Job, we might ask in wonder,
Was there anyone else worthy, to consider?

Job was righteous, and in him, no evil was found.
God blessed him and everything around.
Health and wealth, both were his,
He had everything a man needed, for earthly bliss.
But Satan so cunningly and cleverly did point out.
Job had everything, so why would he, God doubt?
Take away all a man prides in and owns,
Suddenly he wonders if there is a God, and if Him, he knows?!

So Job was tested, stripped of wealth and the ones he loved,
Broken-hearted and in despair, he cried out aloud,
"Naked I came and naked shall I go to God,
He gives, He takes away, Blessed is my Lord!"
God was pleased, for Job, in trial, did not sin,
But Satan simply emphasised, "Skin for skin."
So again, Job was tested, this time with sores,
From head to toe, his body and skin, sores bore.

Friends and family, no one could come to aid.
Their words often caused anger, that lingered and stayed.
Job found himself, filled with pity and pain,
Sorrow over sorrow, over him, seemed to reign.
Elihu then provided them, with rich, comforting, godly words,
Rebuked them for their speech against God, that he had heard.
God is sovereign and over all, supreme, he taught,
Job remembered, and from God, forgiveness he sought.

Oh Job's trial, soon after did fade,
But what a Man of him, it made!
Righteous then and even to this day,
His life, a compass, so in trials, we never stray!
When trials come to you, my friend,
Persevere, be like Job to the end.
To the righteous belong, trials long and hard,
To them also belong, blessings and eternal reward.

Show Me Your Glory!

I have always been fascinated by Moses, his audacity to ask of Yahweh, "Show me your glory!" How bold of him and yet wasn't this the same Moses who was shy and needed a speaker in his brother Aaron, to address Pharaoh? Moses sure came a long way then! From being shy, to asking Yahweh to show him his glory! Also, what a splendid request. It reveals Moses' heart to me; he cared so deeply about Yahweh! Here was a man who spent 40 days and nights, talking with Yahweh and then came back asking to see his glory! What's even more fascinating is, that Yahweh warns, that no man can see his face and live, and Moses requests the same, yet again! The audacity! Was it just audacity? I don't think so; I think he truly loved Yahweh and that's why Yahweh obliged, allowed His goodness to pass before Moses while he stayed in the cleft of a rock! Yahweh made a provision for Moses and granted what had never been done before or since! It thrills my heart that Moses got to spend seconds, minutes, hours, or whatever it was, in the cleft of the rock while Yahweh covered him with his hand! No wonder Deuteronomy ends with *"And there has not arisen a prophet since in Israel like Moses, whom the Lord knew face to face"* – Deuteronomy 34:10. Now as fascinating as that was, Moses in the cleft of the rock, what a beautiful eternity awaits all those who believe in Christ Jesus! There will be no hand over us, blocking our vision! We get to see all of it, everything! The radiance of God will be our forever light; let that sink in!

Exodus 33:17-23

And the Lord said to Moses, "This very thing that you have spoken I will do, for you have found favour in my sight, and I know you by name." Moses said, "Please show me your glory." And he said, "I will make all my goodness pass before you and will proclaim before you my name 'The Lord.' And I will be gracious to whom I will be gracious, and will show mercy on whom I will show mercy. But," he said, "you cannot see my face, for man shall not see me and live." And the Lord said, "Behold, there is a place by me where you shall stand on the rock, and while my glory passes by I will put you in a cleft of the rock, and I will cover you with my hand until I have passed by. Then I will take away my hand, and you shall see my back, but my face shall not be seen."

Revelation 21:11

"Having the glory of God, its radiance like a most rare jewel, like a jasper, clear as crystal."

Revelation 21:23

And the city has no need of sun or moon to shine on it, for the glory of God gives it light, and its lamp is the Lamb.

In the Cleft of the Rock

In the cleft of the rock,
What beauty I see.
In the cleft of the rock,
Safety and protection,
given to me.
In the cleft of the rock
That wondrous face,
Hidden from me.
In the cleft of the rock,
Splendid glory, revealed to me.
In the cleft of the rock,
Just my God and I.
Oh! The cleft in that rock,
The place I seek, to forever lie.
But the cleft in that rock,
Just a shadow of what will be,
When I, in my Father's dwelling, shall be.
That blessed face, no longer hidden from me.
That Splendid glory, my light, forever will be.

In His Strength

Have you ever felt alone, like really alone, even in the midst of a crowd? I have. Have you found yourself wondering how even at church you feel left out? I have. Have you ever felt like you've been beaten down, too many times to count, and that nothing matters anymore? I have! After a series of unfortunate events that took place in my life, I really felt like I had nothing else to lose, like there wasn't anything I found joy in. I was upset, not angry but just indifferent to God. I kept battling with myself over all that I was feeling and all that I knew. Memorising scripture is so precious to me, because honestly, it is what brought me out of this phase. I love that the Bible tells us to examine the word of God, test it! So yes, I debated with myself over scripture. Why do I feel alone? Doesn't scripture say *"He will never leave you nor forsake you?"* Why do I feel overwhelmed by my trial? Doesn't scripture say *"No temptation has seized you except that which is common to man"* and that *"God will give you not more than you can bear"*? Why do I feel like I can't go on? Doesn't scripture say *"My grace is sufficient for you, for my power is made perfect in weakness"*? Why do I feel so rotten when scripture says *"my peace I give to you"*? I wrestled with all of these verses and the more I wrestled, the more scripture flooded my heart. I know that this wasn't the first time I was examining God's word or testing it, I had done it in the past and I found it to be true! Truth doesn't change with time, neither is it relative. So if it was true then, it must be true now also. So what changed then? Me!

In the midst of all my trials I lost track of who is sovereign over my life. That feeling of helplessness was true, simply because I was trying to fight it on my own. Stupidly, I was attempting the impossible. It is a tough lesson to learn, but an important one, our God is a God who grants us good and adversity, trial and peace, joy and sorrow. And as hard as it is to believe, he works all things, the good, the bad, the ugly, all things, for the good of those who love him. During trials, I tend to forget that, but the truth is, I need scripture more than ever, during such times. Scripture helps give me the right view of God and a better view of sinful old me. Scripture reminds me that I was bought with a price and no trial on earth, equals what Christ has already done for me! Also, the words of that beautiful hymn kept coming back to me: "*Let me at Thy throne of mercy, find a sweet relief; Kneeling there in deep contrition, Help my unbelief.*" Even in trial or sinking faith, I have found, that the only thing I know how to do, is go to the Lord in prayer. And I have learnt, even to trust him more, I need him! There is absolutely nothing I can do on my own. Over time I have also learnt, that while that seemed like a terrible, desperate cry, that was still, a great place to be in – to know, only God has the answers even when I am doubtful!

Psalm 73:25-26

Whom have I in heaven but you? And there is nothing on earth that I desire besides you. My flesh and my heart may fail, but God is the strength of my heart and my portion forever.

Ephesians 2"12-13

Remember that you were at that time separated from Christ, alienated from the commonwealth of Israel, and strangers to the covenants of promise, having no hope and without God in the world. 13 But now, in Christ Jesus, you who once were far off have been brought near by the blood of Christ.

Trial

Not more than you can bear, he said,
Yet somehow, the burden I cannot carry.
Not without my peace, he said,
Yet somehow, chaos dwells within me.
Not without my will, he said,
Yet I suffer, sorrow after sorrow.
Not without the Comforter, he said,
Yet all I have, is wounded spirit.
Not on your own, he said,
Yet without help, I cry, weary.
Not for your bad, he said,
Yet the good, I cannot trace.
If all that he said is true,
Shouldn't I feel renewed?
If all that he said is right,
Shouldn't I, in trial, feel alright?
Why, O Lord, does the truth
Not set me free?
Why, O Lord, do my trials
Not let me, your grace see?
In Joy, my praise is ever yours,
In sorrow, I wonder if I am yours.
Give me confidence, Lord, that your word is ever true,
Give me wisdom, Lord, to know my place is on bended knee.

Give me assurance, Lord, that even trials, are from your hand,
Give me belief, Lord, that knows no turn, even when things are
bad.
Open my eyes, Lord, your grace to ever see,
Open my heart, Lord, your slave to ever be,
Open my mind, Lord, to know you've already set me free!

Power of the Cross

Nothing in all of history is as gripping and horrifying as Calvary, because Calvary is the story of a perfect, holy, righteous being, being crucified for sin that you and I committed. What had never ever happened before happened, and it will never ever happen again! Because, once for all, Christ died and gave us sinners free access to God the Father! Calvary covered it all, every terrible sin, the price was paid in full. The book of John is fascinating, the introduction itself is so packed with doctrine, and John introduces us to Christ in Chapter 1 and says of him *"Behold, the Lamb of God, who takes away the sin of the world!"*. Much before Jesus went to the cross, John introduced him as the "Lamb who takes away sin"! Jesus came with one purpose and one purpose alone, to pay for your sin and mine. John even adds affirmation from God the Father *"I myself did not know him, but he who sent me to baptise with water said to me, 'He on whom you see the Spirit descend and remain, this is he who baptises with the Holy Spirit.' And I have seen and have borne witness that this is the Son of God."* And Matthew's account of the same event is even better; he says *"And when Jesus was baptised, immediately he went up from the water, and behold, the heavens were opened to him, and he saw the Spirit of God descending like a dove and coming to rest on him; and behold, a voice from heaven said, "This is my beloved Son with whom I am well pleased."*. God loved his Son; He was pleased with Him, and yet at Calvary, we hear Jesus cry *"My God, my God, why have you forsaken me?"*. It is hard for our finite minds to grasp it all, that a loving Father would send his only Son, who out of love, would give up his life, on a cross, to buy pardon for you and I. Calvary cost the Father and his Son! None of us know of love like that which the Father and Son, have shared from eternity past, to all of eternity! We owe it all to Calvary! We must tell its story now and forevermore!

Hebrews 12:2
Looking to Jesus, the founder and perfecter of our faith, who for the joy that was set before him endured the cross, despising the shame, and is seated at the right hand of the throne of God.

John 3:16-17
"For God so loved the world, that he gave his only Son, that whoever believes in him should not perish but have eternal life. For God did not send his Son into the world to condemn the world, but in order that the world might be saved through him."

1 John 5:11-12
And this is the testimony, that God gave us eternal life, and this life is in his Son. Whoever has the Son has life; whoever does not have the Son of God does not have life.

Cross Hymn

O that I might grasp, that great old love,
unselfish, unconditional, unfailing love.
Which on Calvary's blessed tree,
Purchased my pardon, O so free!

O that I might forever, to that cross cling,
And tell brothers, of salvation it doth bring.
That they might know, Christ in life,
And in death gain, everlasting life.

O might that love and cross, be my guide,
While I through trials, and temptations ride.
O that I might be, its humble slave,
Serve faithfully, till I reach the grave.

Chorus:-
Keep thy cross ever before me,
Let thy love, ever surround me.

Refined

The Christian life is not one of ease. It is one of being refined by fire, much like gold. We are called to live an exemplary life like Christ. While we may claim to do that daily, the truth of our claim is best seen in our endurance during trial. It is indeed all good to say "I believe" when all is well. It is all but easy to say "I believe", when nothing is going our way. Trials are but proof of the claims we make as Christians. I don't know about you, but often enough I have felt sorry for myself, asking why me or why this now, Lord? And in asking that question, I understand I'm exercising a bit of audacity and proclaiming that I am unjustly treated. But really, is that injustice? Is my plight during a trial injustice offered by the Lord? Do I really have the right to say to him who delivered me from death, why this, Lord? Trials are great teachers and they demand humility, because they remind us that we are nothing, but for the grace of God. During a trial, when we feel that wave of anger over our plight, we ought to take a pause and ask ourselves, are we facing more than Christ did? Our answer will always be in the negative. Now, if Christ, holy, pure, and without blemish endured the cross, do you and I really have anything to complain about? Our trial, however big it may be, can never match up to the pure injustice at Calvary. We need to understand this: sin has consequences, the consequence is death, but thanks be to Christ Jesus, who gave himself up for us, so that we might not have to taste eternal damnation. However, the consequence of the existence of sin, will continue to be felt by us all. We will struggle on this side of heaven, that's a given. When we are struggling with trial and sin, we need to look to Calvary; it will help change our perspective. We don't dwell on our pain; we look to him who bore all our pain, so that one day, we will enjoy eternity in a joyful heaven. We look to Christ, because we know, He endured and He gives us strength to endure. Trials are not meant to break us; they are meant to shake the ground beneath us, to remind us that our footing is on solid ground, when our faith is in Christ. Trials are meant to sprout roots that grow deeper in Christ and give us an unshakeable foundation, for our faith, no matter what our circumstance.

James 1:2-3
Count it all joy, my brothers, when you meet trials of various kinds, for you know that the testing of your faith produces steadfastness.

1 Peter 4:12
Beloved, do not be surprised at the fiery trial when it comes upon you to test you, as though something strange were happening to you.

Romans 8:16-17
The Spirit himself bears witness with our spirit that we are children of God, and if children, then heirs—heirs of God and fellow heirs with Christ, provided we suffer with him in order that we may also be glorified with him.

The Promise of Trial

To trial, I am no stranger.
No foreigner, to heartbreak.
Sorrow has been
Both, foe and friend,
Tears I've shed, without end.
Such is the life I was born into,
Is such the life, Christ meant?

More losses than wins, for a while,
More illness than health, walk beside.
Long days of wants I cannot have,
Long nights of fears I cannot share.
Such is the life I keep living,
Is such the life that's Christlike?

For mortal men, time is measure,
Earth is home, this life, our treasure.
But time, loses power with Christ.
"Perfect" is, his only measure,
Sanctified children, his only pleasure.
God gives to each, as he deems fit,
Trial and faith, they are intricately knit.
What we might count, as lack of love,
Is but God's intimate pruning, for our prize above.
He does not unfairly decree pain,

Christ suffered and showed us, that loss is gain.
Our saviour, high priest, precious friend,
He guides and intercedes for us, to the end.

So is trial what we must face?
Indeed, it is. In trial, we find our place.
We do not count, wins and losses,
We do not dwell, on our pain.
We remember the cross and all its evil,
We rejoice in deliverance, from the devil.
We recognize grace, that much, has been given,
More than we need, on this side of heaven.
We look to Christ through the tears we shed,
We beg him, to keep us walking, in his step.
And hard as our trial, may prove to be,
Calvary assures, he delivers me.
And one day, we will fully know and see,
Trials, it worked out; all good for you and me.

Seek Ye First

I've loved that chorus "Seek ye first the kingdom of God" since I was a kid, but what's even better is that the chorus echoes the truth of the Bible. In several places in the Bible, we have been told that this world isn't our home; this isn't the place to spend our time seeking things. Our home is in heaven, where Christ is, and we are all headed there if we believe in him. Seeking heaven is about seeking after him who is seated in heaven, Christ Jesus. We are called to be like him; that is our purpose here on earth. We are called to love God and God alone, while here on earth and seek to be like him! Seeking to be like him means denying self and following Christ's example. It means treasuring Christ above all else or anyone else.

The word "seek" suggests an active looking. Have you ever lost your keys, right before you have to set out? You look with desperation for it, right? especially when you're running late! That's the idea, we seek God like we would seek our keys, if they were lost. And to those who seek after Christ with that enthusiasm, with that desperation and longing, to them, he forever remains found! He blesses that desire. He gives to them what they seek!

Matthew 6: 19-21
"Do not lay up for yourselves treasures on earth, where moth and rust destroy and where thieves break in and steal, but lay up for yourselves treasures in heaven, where neither moth nor rust

destroys and where thieves do not break in and steal. For where your treasure is, there your heart will be also."

Colossians 3:1-5

If then you have been raised with Christ, seek the things that are above, where Christ is seated at the right hand of God. Set your minds on things that are above, not on things that are on earth. For you have died, and your life is hidden with Christ in God. When Christ who is your life appears, then you also will appear with him in glory. Put to death therefore what is earthly in you.

Hebrews 1:1-3

Long ago, at many times and in many ways, God spoke to our fathers by the prophets, but in these last days he has spoken to us by his Son, whom he appointed the heir of all things, through whom also he created the world. He is the radiance of the glory of God and the exact imprint of his nature, and he upholds the universe by the word of his power. After making purification for sins, he sat down at the right hand of the Majesty on high.

Treasures in Heaven

What has this world to offer but riches and gold?
What else so dear, than wealth to hold?

Riches they fade not and hence acclaimed,
Diamonds and rubies will forever be famed.

But what with these riches, so easily rusted,
Not even your closest friend, with them can be trusted.

So precious are they, that all want to steal,
Love for it so strong, no one can heal.

Money and God, we both, can't serve,
For our dear Lord, true heart does deserve.

For what your heart does choose to treasure,
In that, will it indeed, find true pleasure!

Our Father in heaven has promised us more,
If we true treasures, in heaven, will store.

The treasures in heaven, far richer than gold,
For in Christ, we do have, eternal wealth untold.

Living Through Loss

2017 was a difficult year, more loss than I was prepared for. My Godmother had long suffered from kidney failure and finally breathed her last in July. She was a fighter, if resilience was personified, it would look just like her. I always assumed, she'd always simply stay, fighting. A few months later, we lost my eldest uncle in December, again a huge blow to me. The best way to describe my uncle would be – More a friend, less an uncle, at most times, more a Dad, less an uncle, when I needed one. Losing my uncle was even harder because I was tucked in a corner, on the other side of the world and couldn't even make it back in time, for his funeral. On most days, I can control my emotions fairly well, but hearing he was gone brought me to tears instantly. If this loss wasn't hard enough, I had a tonne of ailments that year. At church, every 31st Dec night, we have time given to reflect and share what happened in the year. While living through December, I remember thinking to myself, I am going to have nothing worthy to share. How in the world do I say, 2017 was a good year when I lost two people I loved? And then on the 29th of December, I sat next to my best friend at a wedding, and he was asking for an update on my recent travels, health, etc. and to my surprise, after hearing my latest update on my health and of course he knew about my losses, he turned to me and said, "Bro, God really loves you." I was stunned for a minute. I wanted to ask him, were you listening to everything I said? But I was also stunned because this was my friend who rarely spoke of God, telling me God loved me.

He saw my puzzled look and went on to say, "Bro, for the last few years I have seen insane things happen with your health and going by the doctor's words and just science, you shouldn't be here. You should have died some time ago, yet here you are." Ron always knew how to cheer me, but I never thought he would be the one who reminds me of God's love. The next poem was born from the reassurance I received at that wedding when Ron reminded me that God loved me. Trials are not meant only to hurt us or cause us trouble; they are also meant to make us know of God's love. In our trial, we are never alone; He is with us.

Hebrews 13:5
For he has said, "I will never leave you nor forsake you."

Hebrews 12:5-6
And Have you forgotten the exhortation that addresses you as sons?
"My son, do not regard lightly the discipline of the Lord,
nor be weary when reproved by him.
For the Lord disciplines the one he loves,
and chastises every son whom he receives."

Confessions

This year has finally gone by.
And Oh! It's been such hell,
I've cried a million tears,
Though not even a friend
Or foe can tell.
For I mask my heart well.
And to the world pretend, all is swell.
But inside, I am eaten and torn,
My soul's weary, I'm bitter and worn.
And if all this pain is still incomparable to hell,
Mustn't I the world, of Jesus tell?
Oh, brother, if the pain of which I speak of, you already know,
Imagine, hell will be a thousandfold more.
Oh! sister, if this pain is more than you can take,
Imagine hell, where you pay for every sin and mistake.
Oh! That you, my family, may find Christ,
In Him, peace and mercy, for everyone, even the despised.
He knows of the pain you and I bear.
He knows far more than you and I, can ever share.
Calvary, a price he paid, for you and me,
He died, so you and I, from hell, can be free.
So why bear your burdens, like you have no saviour?
Why cry as if there is no redemption?
Instead humbly, to him approach, and receive salvation.
Let this world, be the only hell, you know,

Your next life, in his presence, live forevermore.
And while we are here on earth,
Living the days ordained for us from birth,
Let us cast our every tear on him.
Knowing, He can cheer our hearts,
Even when all around, the light grows dim.
Let us trust him to be our shepherd and guide.
Who better to instruct us, than one who walks beside.
Let us to him, draw near, whether in good or bad times,
Knowing full well, he is sovereign, at all times.
And until our time is finally done here,
May we always find true - Christ is near!

Colours to Cheer

I've always been a fan of colours but I probably learnt to appreciate it more in nature when confined to the house during Covid. I longed for the colours of nature, when all I had to do was be stuck at home within the four walls. That, eventually led to me growing a lot of flowering plants on my balcony. I love looking out my window and seeing colour; it simply brightens up my mood. Watching a colourful sky, Ah! Nothing can thrill me more. My phone is filled with pictures of sunsets and sunrises from different places, but far more exciting to me than those beautiful horizons, is the opportunity to see and capture a rainbow! The seven colours forming a bow in the sky are simply glorious, and how wonderful it is that this gorgeous treat, is nothing but the sign, that God uses as a covenant with Man? The rainbow, whenever it appears, is a reminder to God of his covenant to never wipe off men from the surface of the earth. In Genesis Chapter 8, we read that God reveals "the intentions of man's heart are evil from youth," which means men will sin like Noah's time, and yet God is gracious and has made this covenant with us, to never again wipe out, all living creatures from earth. How kind is this God? How amazing is his heart, that despite knowing we will sin and cause him grief, he makes a promise to us, where the cost of it is paid by him alone? He gives, without asking for anything in return. Rainbows thrill my heart; it also reminds me that the God of Noah is alive and remembers me. He is watching; what more could I possibly want?

Genesis 6:5-8

The Lord saw that the wickedness of man was great in the earth, and that every intention of the thoughts of his heart was only evil continually. 6 And the Lord regretted that he had made man on the earth, and it grieved him to his heart. 7 So the Lord said, "I will blot out man whom I have created from the face of the land, man and animals and creeping things and birds of the heavens, for I am sorry that I have made them." 8 But Noah found favour in the eyes of the Lord.

Genesis 9: 9-14

When I bring clouds over the earth and the bow is seen in the clouds, I will remember my covenant that is between me and you and every living creature of all flesh. And the waters shall never again become a flood to destroy all flesh. When the bow is in the clouds, I will see it and remember the everlasting covenant between God and every living creature of all flesh that is on the earth." God said to Noah, "This is the sign of the covenant that I have established between me and all flesh that is on the earth."

Rainbow

There's a rainbow in the sky,
Have you ever wondered why?
It is the sign of blessed hope,
To let you know, with trials, you can cope.

There's a rainbow in the sky,
While the storm refuses to die.
It shines with bright, rich hue,
To let you know, the Bible is ever true.

There's a rainbow in the sky,
Even when the earth is still dry.
For God sends to his people a sign,
Remember, in rain or sunshine, you are mine.

There's a rainbow in the sky,
It makes me fix my eyes on high!
I feel what Noah must have felt,
I know, Yahweh is in control of all I'm dealt.

There's a rainbow in the sky,
'Tis that covenant that shall never die.
For as long as the sky shall hold a bow,
Yahweh shall deliver me, now and evermore.